EDITIONS

ARMENIAN
BATAK/INDONESIAN
BRITISH SIGN
BULGARIAN
BURMESE (Myanmar)
CHINESE
ENGLISH
- Africa
- Australia
- Chinese/English
- India
- Indonesia
- Japan
- Korean/English
- Korean/English/Japanese
- Myanmar
- Philippines
- Singapore
- Sri Lanka
- United Kingdom
- United States

ESTONIAN
FRENCH
GREEK
GUJARATI
HINDI
HUNGARIAN
IBAN/ENGLISH
ILOKANO
INDONESIAN
ITALIAN
JAPANESE
KANNADA
KISWAHILI
KOREAN
MALAYALAM
NEPALI
NORWEGIAN
ODIA
POLISH
PORTUGUESE
- Africa
- Brazil
- Portugal

RUSSIAN
SINHALA
SPANISH
- Caribbean
- Mexico
- South America
- United States

SWEDISH
TAMIL
TELUGU
THAI
URDU

THE UPPER ROOM

WHERE THE WORLD MEETS TO PRAY

Daniele Och
UK editor

INVITATIONAL
INTERDENOMINATIONAL
INTERNATIONAL

36 LANGUAGES

Multiple formats are available in some languages

The Bible Reading Fellowship
15 The Chambers, Vineyard
Abingdon OX14 3FE
brf.org.uk

The Bible Reading Fellowship (BRF) is a Registered Charity (233280)

ISBN 978 1 80039 014 0

Acknowledgements

Scripture quotations marked with the following abbreviations are taken from the version shown. Where no acronym is given, the quotation is taken from the same version as the headline reference.

NIV: The Holy Bible, New International Version (Anglicised edition) copyright © 1979, 1984, 2011 by Biblica. Used by permission of Hodder & Stoughton Publishers, an Hachette UK company. All rights reserved. 'NIV' is a registered trademark of Biblica. UK trademark number 1448790.

KJV: the Authorised Version of the Bible (The King James Bible), the rights in which are vested in the Crown, are reproduced by permission of the Crown's Patentee, Cambridge University Press.

NRSV: The New Revised Standard Version of the Bible, Anglicised Edition, copyright © 1989, 1995 by the Division of Christian Education of the National Council of the Churches of Christ in the USA. Used by permission. All rights reserved.

CEB: copyright © 2011 by Common English Bible.

A catalogue record for this book is available from the British Library

Printed by Gutenberg Press, Tarxien, Malta

How to use *The Upper Room*

The Upper Room is ideal in helping us spend a quiet time with God each day. Each daily entry is based on a passage of scripture and is followed by a meditation and prayer. Each person who contributes a meditation to the magazine seeks to relate their experience of God in a way that will help those who use *The Upper Room* every day.

Here are some guidelines to help you make best use of *The Upper Room*:

1. Read the passage of scripture. It is a good idea to read it more than once, in order to have a fuller understanding of what it is about and what you can learn from it.
2. Read the meditation. How does it relate to your own experience? Can you identify with what the writer has outlined from their own experience or understanding?
3. Pray the written prayer. Think about how you can use it to relate to people you know or situations that need your prayers today.
4. Think about the contributor who has written the meditation. Some users of the *The Upper Room* include this person in their prayers for the day.
5. Meditate on the 'Thought for the day' and the 'Prayer focus', perhaps using them again as the focus for prayer or direction for action.

Why is it important to have a daily quiet time? Many people will agree that it is the best way of keeping in touch every day with the God who sustains us and who sends us out to do his will and show his love to the people we encounter each day. Meeting with God in this way reassures us of his presence with us, helps us to discern his will for us and makes us part of his worldwide family of Christian people through our prayers.

I hope that you will be encouraged as you use the magazine regularly as part of your daily devotions, and that God will richly bless you as you read his word and seek to learn more about him.

Daniele Och
UK editor

BRF needs you!

If you're one of our thousands of regular *Upper Room* readers, you will know all about the impact that regular Bible reading has on your faith and the value of daily notes to encourage and inspire you. *Upper Room* readers share those blessings with Christians across the world; they know that every day, in each part of the day, someone, somewhere is reading the same meditation.

If you enjoy reading *The Upper Room*, and love the feeling of being part of a worldwide family, would you be willing to share your experience with others? Perhaps you could give a short talk or write a brief article about why you find *The Upper Room* so helpful. You could form an *Upper Room* reading group, either face-to-face with friends or colleagues, or online. Or you could pass on your back copies or give someone a gift subscription. However you do it, the important thing is to find creative ways to put a copy of *The Upper Room* into someone else's hands.

It doesn't need to be complicated, and we can help with group and bulk-buy discounts.

We can supply further information if you need it and would love to hear about it if you do find ways to get *The Upper Room* into new readers' hands.

For more information:

- Email **enquiries@brf.org.uk**
- Telephone BRF on **+44 (0)1865 319700** Mon–Fri 9.30–17.00
- Write to us at BRF, 15 The Chambers, Vineyard, Abingdon OX14 3FE

Wait and hope

The angel said to the women, 'Do not be afraid, for I know that you are looking for Jesus, who was crucified. He is not here; he has risen.'
Matthew 28:5–6 (NIV)

As I write this, our world is facing a pandemic. Uncertainty about the immediate future is spreading nearly as fast as the disease, alternately taking root as panic or denial. Vast numbers of people are quarantined to help slow the spread of the virus. Right now the future is unclear, and we are newly aware of the fragile nature of life.

While the themes of uncertainty and the fragility of life have greater weight at this moment than at other times, they are not new. Many writers in this issue speak about seeking God's guidance as they make life-altering decisions or receive a fearsome diagnosis. Some recall wondering as young people what shape their lives would take. Others write about being surprised when they faced roadblocks along the path that they had chosen or had to change course entirely. Through it all, however, each writer tells of God's unfailing presence.

How fitting, then, that we will soon be entering the season of Lent. In the days leading up to Jesus' death, the disciples surely experienced confusion, fear and denial as they followed Jesus into an uncertain future. As we walk with Jesus and the disciples towards Jerusalem and towards the cross, we experience their confusion and fear. Where are we going? What will happen? How will we go on without our beloved teacher? But when the questions become too numerous or the fears threaten to overwhelm us, the gospel reminds us that hope waits beyond the cross. Death is not the final word. This moment is not the only moment. There is hope of new life ahead. And in each moment, our loving God walks with us.

Lindsay L. Gray
Editorial Director, The Upper Room

Where the world meets to pray

Democratic Republic of the Congo
The Upper Room is now available in Kiswahili! This edition is produced by the East Congo Episcopal Area, United Methodist Church, publishing team.

Editions of *The Upper Room* daily devotional guide are printed in:

- Angola
- Côte d'Ivoire
- Democratic Republic of the Congo
- South Africa

Gifts to the international editions of *The Upper Room* help the world meet to pray.
upperroom.org/gift

The editor writes...

‘The virgin will conceive and give birth to a son, and they will call him Immanuel’ (which means ‘God with us’).

Matthew 1:23 (NIV)

Thinking about what to write for my first editorial for *The Upper Room*, I was initially reluctant to mention Covid. The US editors, Lindsay and Andrew, already had wise words to share (see pages 5 and 67), and I was not sure there was anything I could add to them, nor to the many reflections on the pandemic that most of you will have already read and heard.

But then, as I was reading again the guidelines on using *The Upper Room* that are listed at the beginning of each issue (see page 3), some words resonated with me. Long-term readers of these notes will probably skip over this page each issue, as I have often done. This time, however, I noticed the following regarding the importance of a daily quiet time: ‘Meeting with God in this way reassures us of *his presence with us*...’

For me, the dominant theme that has emerged from this year of lockdown and social distancing is the importance of *presence*. While video calls and other technology have been a blessing in enabling people to continue to see and hear their loved ones and participate in communal activities, there is nothing like being actually present with those we care about. It did not take the pandemic to make me realise this, but being compelled to self-isolate did show me how much I take for granted the gift of being present with others.

And it has given me a new appreciation for what it means that God is present with us. The reason that a daily quiet time of reading the Bible reassures us of God’s presence is because the whole book is about our creator God longing – indeed dying – to be *with* us.

God’s love for us is such that he does not settle for a video call or text chat; God wants to be present with us, to dwell with us, to meet with us face to face. The ultimate expression of this is, of course, Jesus – the one who is known as ‘God with us’.

Daniele Och
UK editor

The Bible readings are selected with great care, and we urge you to include the suggested reading in your devotional time.

The junk drawer

Read Luke 9:1–6

It is for freedom that Christ has set us free. Stand firm, then, and do not let yourselves be burdened again by a yoke of slavery.
Galatians 5:1 (NIV)

Every time I opened the junk drawer in my kitchen, I became stressed out and frustrated. I could never find what I needed, and the clutter was unbearable. Finally one day I decided to clean out that jam-packed drawer. In doing so, I discovered that I was holding on to a lot of unnecessary items that I had tossed into the drawer because 'I might need that later' or 'I just can't give that up' or 'I don't know what to do with this.' In reality, I didn't need those things at all, and they ended up as burdens – making the drawer a cluttered mess.

In life I carry around my own personal junk drawer filled with harboured hurts, worries, shame, sin – you name it. I lug it around every day, avoiding dealing with the contents but also refusing to let them go.

Reading today's quoted scripture, I realised that for me the yoke of slavery was symbolised by the clutter of my junk drawer. Now, every time I open my newly cleaned drawer, I remember that I don't have to hold on to sin, shame and anger because living with Christ has set me free.

Prayer: *Father God, help us rid our lives of harboured hurts and needless fears that keep us from the joy of your abundant life. Your son has set us free; help us to walk in that freedom. In Jesus' name. Amen*

Thought for the day: Christ sets me free to live with abundant joy.

Maddie Falk (Texas, US)

 PRAYER FOCUS: SOMEONE HANGING ON TO AN OLD HURT

Perseverance

Read Isaiah 40:28–31

Those who hope in the Lord will renew their strength. They will soar on wings like eagles; they will run and not grow weary, they will walk and not be faint.

Isaiah 40:31 (NIV)

When I was younger and rode my bicycle long distances, the lesson of today's quoted verse was made very real to me. I remember seeing hills in the distance that appeared to be nearly vertical and impossible to pedal over. The mirage of the looming challenge stirred apprehension and dread in my mind, and I entertained thoughts of quitting and turning around to go home. But I always made the decision to forge ahead and confront the situation. Each time, to my surprise and delight, the impossibility of the climb evaporated as I started to ride up the hill. The steepness of the road melted away, and I was emboldened with the confidence to conquer the challenge. The ride required much effort, but with one pedal stroke after another I accomplished my goal and a sense of achievement and confidence blossomed.

How many times in our lives has each of us encountered a 'steep hill'? With a strong faith in God and a personal resolve to see a task or difficulty through, we all can overcome obstacles that at first may cause us to recoil. But each victory we achieve strengthens us. As we strengthen our faith so as to move mountains, we can imbue others around us with the same strength.

Prayer: *Dear Lord, grant us the strength and peace that comes from faith in Jesus Christ so that we will not shrink from obligations and opportunities we face each day. Amen*

Thought for the day: God can help me persevere to reach my goals.

Craig Sanford (Kansas, US)

In every circumstance

Read Habakkuk 3:16–19

As for me, I watch in hope for the Lord, I wait for God my Saviour; my God will hear me.

Micah 7:7 (NIV)

One of my favorite scripture passages is Habakkuk's prayer. The passage became personal for me on the day my car battery malfunctioned on my way home. I stopped in the parking lot of the local shopping centre because it had started to rain. It was getting dark, my daughters and I were hungry and I had hardly any money – not even enough to make a phone call.

I approached some police officers to ask them to call my husband, and when I returned to my car I prayed out loud to God. Soon people gathered around us offering help. God's presence was evident during this stressful moment. Although the problem was not yet resolved, I began to experience a sense of calm.

Being faithful does not simply mean attending church services and singing hymns every Sunday. It means praising and looking for God in every circumstance, no matter how bleak.

Habakkuk was in deep anguish and still prayed and praised God. Habakkuk reminds us to wait patiently. God did not forget the prophet, and God will not forget us.

Prayer: *Faithful God, help us to remember that we are yours when chaos descends on us. Strengthen our resolve to praise you in all circumstances. In Jesus' name. Amen*

Thought for the day: In moments of crisis, I will remain strong and praise God.

Angélica Afú (Panama)

God's blessings

Read Psalm 103:1–8

Bless the Lord, O my soul: and all that is within me, bless his holy name. Bless the Lord, O my soul, and forget not all his benefits.
Psalm 103:1–2 (KJV)

Today's quoted verses were my childhood pastor's favourite opening greeting to our small, rural congregation. He worked as a church planter and started many churches throughout the 1950s, 60s and 70s. I was one of the first he baptised in that church when I was eight years old, and he preached the gospel to me throughout my childhood. The church is now large, and that pastor has long since passed on.

Today, my soul praises the holy name of the Lord for the many Christian congregations that have prayed for me throughout my life, from the church and pastor of my faith's beginnings to the loving congregation currently blessing me and my loved ones. The Lord's blessings are many. When we recount them in our hearts with gratitude, these blessings encourage us in all circumstances and help us rejoice in God's abundance in the past and in our continuing blessings.

Prayer: *Dear Lord, thank you for the many blessings you have sent throughout our lives and for all blessings yet to come. We pray as Jesus taught us, 'Father, hallowed be your name, your kingdom come. Give us each day our daily bread. Forgive us our sins, for we also forgive everyone who sins against us. And lead us not into temptation.'* Amen*

Thought for the day: Remembering past blessings with gratitude strengthens me for today.

Gary E. Crum (Virginia, US)

PRAYER FOCUS: PASTORS OF RURAL CHURCHES

*Luke 11:2–4 (NIV)

Meeting with God

Read 1 Corinthians 2:9–16

There, above the cover between the two cherubim that are over the ark of the covenant law, I will meet with you and give you all my commands for the Israelites.

Exodus 25:22 (NIV)

I was in my 20s and working in the IT department of a hospital. The department was located in the basement of the multistorey car park, so I took walks at lunchtime to get out in the sun. I often walked to the chapel at the hospital, which is where I first found *The Upper Room*. As a new Christian, I hungered to meet with God and to hear God's voice, and God spoke to me through this publication and the Bible.

Today I still have that hunger, and God continues to speak to me through this devotional guide and the Bible. I read it every morning during my quiet time. I pray, 'Please, Lord, speak to me through your word.' And the Lord does!

In the scripture quoted above, Moses met with God at the ark. Thankfully today we have God's Spirit living in us, allowing us to meet with God throughout the day, every day. God is our source of love, forgiveness, encouragement, teaching and direction. I hope to continue growing in the practice of praying and meeting God throughout the day.

Prayer: *Dear Father, thank you for your word and your Holy Spirit. Thank you for allowing us to come to you at any time and for giving us ears and hearts to hear when you speak to us. In Jesus' name. Amen*

Thought for the day: I can meet with God all day, every day.

Irene E. Chomicki (Texas, US)

 PRAYER FOCUS: THOSE WHO WORK IN INFORMATION TECHNOLOGY

Choosing a path

Read Proverbs 16:1–9

In their hearts humans plan their course, but the Lord establishes their steps.

Proverbs 16:9 (NIV)

For a long time I believed that there was only one clear path for my life and that if I missed it, I would be out of God's perfect will for me. But I think that obeying God is not that clear-cut. I now believe God has given us interests and talents in areas that will bring us a joyful life. Surely we have a say in the outcome, but I believe God can bless anything we put our hands and hearts to as long as we are seeking God. Proverbs 16:9 says, 'In their hearts humans plan their course, but the Lord establishes their steps.'

What liberating words! When I faithfully plan a course of action, God will be with me every step of the way. God has given me talents and desires; it is up to me to use them. I was always afraid that God would call me to go somewhere I didn't want to go – to preach the gospel there. Maybe someday God will; but I also believe that God will place a desire in my heart to do so. For now, I just want to use the talents God has given me and minister in the circles I live in, remembering that God wants the best for me.

Prayer: *O God, thank you for gifts and talents we can use to joyfully serve your people. Amen*

Thought for the day: God blesses my acts of service.

George Peters (British Columbia, Canada)

PRAYER FOCUS: SOMEONE UNSURE OF HOW TO SERVE GOD

A good night's sleep

Read Psalm 4

I will praise the Lord, who counsels me; even at night my heart instructs me.

Psalm 16:7 (NIV)

In the past, sleep sometimes eluded me. Though I would try to relax, I would replay conversations from the day and consider how I might have responded differently. Sometimes I would fret about a difficult situation at work or the health of a loved one.

As my faith grew, I realised such brooding was counterproductive – God was calling me to focus on positive things (see Philippians 4:8). I started what I now call my 'blessing book'. At the beginning of each year, I purchase a weekly planner with several lines for each day. Before going to bed I spend a few minutes reflecting on the day – its accomplishments, challenges and blessings – and list things for which I am thankful. These blessings can be as ordinary as a call from a friend or as remarkable as recovering from surgery. When I'm concerned about something, I make a note to remind me that God is in control and prayerfully turn the situation over to the Lord. As I write, I give thanks for the many ways I encounter God's love.

Lately it has become common for me to start my list of blessings with 'a good night's sleep'. My night-time anxiety has been exchanged for the peace only God can give.

Prayer: *God of peace, thank you for the gift of rest. Help us to trust you with our worries. Amen*

Thought for the day: Counting my blessings can bring me peace.

Lisa Stackpole (Wisconsin, US)

Plugged in

Read 1 John 1:5–10

The sun shall no longer be your light by day, nor for brightness shall the moon give light to you by night; but the Lord will be your everlasting light, and your God will be your glory.

Isaiah 60:19 (NRSV)

'That's a good start to the weekend. This kettle is faulty; it won't switch on!' I looked up from unpacking the suitcase. After a long drive to the hotel, my husband was trying to make a cup of tea. He left the kettle and went to plug in his phone charger. 'There's no electricity!' he said.

I sighed. Then I noticed that the key fob was not in the slot by the door. It had to be inserted and remain in place for the electricity supply to work. Apparent fault rectified, my husband soon had his cup of tea.

The episode made me think of our relationship with God. Many people 'plug in' to God when in need or want, but don't bother when things are running smoothly. God desires us to leave our key – our trust in him – in place at all times. This ensures us unlimited access to his love and almighty power.

Prayer: *Father God, forgive us for neglecting you when things are going well. Help us to remain in you at all times; seeking you in the good times as well as the bad. Amen*

Thought for the day: God's power supply is always on.

Julia Cutting (England, United Kingdom)

The God who cares

Read 1 Peter 5:1–10

Cast all your anxiety on [God] because he cares for you.

1 Peter 5:7 (NIV)

While preparing to plant cassava (*Manihot esculenta*), I had to clear tall grass from the plot of land. I decided to burn the partially green and partially dried grass. Because it was not a dry season, I thought this would be safe, but the fire burned much faster than I expected. I began to panic as the fire threatened to engulf the neighbouring plots of land. Frantically, I threw sand on the fire to put it out. The smoke was choking me.

Then I remembered to call on the Lord. I prayed through the panic: 'Lord, help me; you always help me when I ask. Please don't let this fire cross the boundaries.' The fire eventually died down, and I lifted my hands and thanked God.

Anxiety is a natural response to misfortune and danger. When we hold on to our anxiety and allow it to overwhelm us, fear may keep us from being able to think calmly or trust God.

Today's verse reminds us that we can cast our fears on the Lord. In times of anxiety, we can trust that the God who cares for us will move to help us solve our problems.

Prayer: *Dear God, help us when we cast our anxiety on you. In Jesus' name. Amen*

Thought for the day: I can give my anxiety to God.

Charity M. Kiregyera (Kampala, Uganda)

 PRAYER FOCUS: SOMEONE WHO IS ANXIOUS

Take heart

Read Galatians 6:1–9

If we hope for what we do not see, we wait for it with patience.
Romans 8:25 (NRSV)

As a teenager, I would wake my sister every Sunday morning and ask, ‘Do you want to go to church with me?’ She always said no, but then one day she said yes. So then I started asking, ‘Will you go on a mission trip with me?’ Again, she kept saying no until one day she said yes. While we were in Haiti, my mentor, who knew how much I had wanted my sister to be part of the church, gave me a hug and said, ‘You did it.’

But you see, I didn’t do anything; God did. I was just a voice for God. Every Sunday morning that I asked my sister to come to church and she declined, God was one week closer to having another child in the kingdom and was smiling. As my mentor congratulated me, I realised that God was also thanking me for trusting God’s timing. Every new ‘no’ for me might be one less ‘no’ for God. I just need to trust God’s timing.

We don’t always get an immediate answer from God, but it is our duty to serve God and do God’s will even when we can’t yet see God’s plans or gifts. God has an answer; we may just need to give it more time.

Prayer: *Dear God, provide us with the endurance to do your will and the patience to wait on your timing. Amen*

Thought for the day: Today I will trust God’s timing.

Rachel Turner (Texas, US)

Stretch out your hand

Read Exodus 14:15–22

Then Moses stretched out his hand over the sea, and all that night the Lord drove the sea back… and turned it into dry land… and the Israelites went through the sea on dry ground.

Exodus 14:21–22 (NIV)

The year 2018 was one of enormous change for me. My daughter was born, and both of my grandmothers died within a three-month period. After constant prayer I came to the conclusion that the best way to find peace and rest is to always raise our hands in praise and prayer to God.

When the Egyptians were closing in on the Israelites after Moses led them out of Egypt, God commanded Moses to raise his staff and stretch out his hand over the sea to part the waters. After decades in bondage and slavery it would have been easy for Moses to decline in fatigue, doubt or anger. Instead of allowing the situation to defeat him and his people, Moses chose to listen to God. He raised his staff and stretched his hand over the water. This one act of obedience opened the window for a miracle and delivered the Israelites from the hands of Pharaoh.

When we choose to worship God no matter our circumstances, God can do things that to the world seem impossible. No matter how exhausted we are under the weight of our struggle, God does not want us to despair. God is with us as we persevere.

Prayer: *Faithful God, give us the strength to lift our hands to you when we are weak from struggle. Amen*

Thought for the day: I can praise God through my struggles.

Zach Schaar (Ohio, US)

 PRAYER FOCUS: SOMEONE FEELING EXHAUSTED

A knock at the door

Read Isaiah 65:17–25

Ask and it will be given to you; seek and you will find; knock and the door will be opened to you.

Matthew 7:7 (NIV)

Growing up in the suburbs of London, I remember mischievous children knocking at our door and running off before my mother had time to open it. She would be puzzled and then upset that her work had been interrupted. When I moved to a new town as an adult, I experienced the same prank and discovered how frustrating it was to open the door to find no one there.

For many years I tried to lead my life without God's guidance. Finally, when everything fell apart, a wise Christian friend suggested I pray to God for help. Somewhat sceptically, I 'knocked' in prayer and to my amazement discovered God's door opened to me. With God's help and the assistance of Christian friends, I got my life on track. Over the years I have come to trust that when I knock at God's door, God will always open it to me.

I wonder if there are times when I am like the children playing their game. When have I knocked at God's door in prayer but not waited around long enough to hear an answer? Does God open the door to find I have vanished? The miracle of grace is that God constantly listens for our knocking and always responds in love by being there for us.

Prayer: *Heavenly Father, grant us perseverance and persistence in prayer. Amen*

Thought for the day: God always responds when I call.

Faith Ford (England, United Kingdom)

Encountering God

Read Psalm 34:4–19

Many are the afflictions of the righteous, but the Lord rescues them from them all.

Psalm 34:19 (NRSV)

During my senior year of college, all was well in my world. I planned to go to seminary and to marry my college sweetheart. But then she broke up with me. A few days later my marine corps reserve unit was activated to go to Iraq, and I was told to be ready for an 18-month deployment. At the same time, I had a delay in receiving my commission as a navy chaplain.

I felt rejected and alone, so I got on my knees and prayed. Right after praying, an idea came to me – I could work with my professors to accelerate my graduation before going to Iraq. By the grace of God, I was able to graduate early, I was accepted to seminary, and shortly after that I received my commission as a navy chaplain. Then my marine corps reserve unit called to tell me that my position for deployment wasn't needed.

We all experience rejection and loneliness. While David was on the run from Saul, he must have felt rejected and lonely (see 1 Samuel 21—24). However, in today's reading, we see that David's relationship with God reassured him that God had not forsaken him but was close and wanted him to have salvation. And the same is true for us.

Prayer: *Lord Jesus, help us to follow your example and draw close to God, even when it seems like our world is falling apart. Amen*

Thought for the day: Today, I will remember that God is with me in my troubles.

Rosario 'Roz' Picardo (Ohio, US)

A butterfly's lesson

Read Jeremiah 18:1–6

Do not conform to the pattern of this world, but be transformed by the renewing of your mind. Then you will be able to test and approve what God's will is – his good, pleasing and perfect will.

Romans 12:2 (NIV)

I once had the opportunity to visit a butterfly garden, where I saw a variety of species of butterflies with their beautiful shades of colour and differing sizes. I thought about the various stages through which these insects must pass to reach adulthood and become butterflies.

As I meditated on this image, I stopped to think about our spiritual life. We too must experience transformation in order to renew ourselves, to grow and to share our faith with others by showing what God does in our lives. As followers of Jesus, we become 'the light of the world' and the 'salt of the earth' (Matthew 5:13–14). Our words and actions are transformed!

How do we experience such a transformation? Through a life of intimacy with God – by reading God's word, by praying and by serving in Jesus' name. Just as nature renews itself every season, our spiritual life will be renewed when we follow the way of Christ.

Prayer: *Transform us, Lord! Search us and change our whole being, giving us a new and sanctified life. In the name of Jesus. Amen*

Thought for the day: Christ has the power to change my life.

Carolina Maia Faria (Minas Gerais, Brazil)

PRAYER FOCUS: FOR SPIRITUAL RENEWAL

Light of the world

Read John 1:1–9

When Jesus spoke again to the people, he said, 'I am the light of the world. Whoever follows me will never walk in darkness, but will have the light of life.'
John 8:12 (NIV)

Recently I had a blackout blind installed in my room. Generally it is very efficient, but the blind still lets a sliver of light through the top and down the sides. At night, when it is of course much darker outside, turning off the artificial lights makes the room seem as though it is totally dark. Within a short space of time, however, as my eyes adjust to the darkness, the peripheral light becomes more visible and soon is quite noticeable.

This made me think about the contrast between darkness and light in the Christian life. In the darkness of difficult circumstances that sometimes seem to overwhelm us, there is still a sliver of light shining. Physically, I wanted the darkness to be complete, so that I could sleep better. Spiritually, however, instead of concentrating on the darkness, I and other Christians want to focus on the light of God's presence.

Prayer, praise, Bible reading and meditation, and fellowship with other Christians all help us to develop a deeper and stronger relationship with our loving heavenly Father.

Prayer: *Lord, you came to this world to bring us the light of your truth. Help us to keep close to you, that we may grow to know and serve you better day by day. Amen*

Thought for the day: God is always there to enlighten us and show us the way ahead.

Christine Hay (Scotland, United Kingdom)

 PRAYER FOCUS: THOSE WHO DO NOT KNOW JESUS AS THE LIGHT OF LIFE

Rainbow promises

Read Genesis 9:12–17

Those who stand firm during testing are blessed... They will receive the life God has promised to those who love him as their reward.
James 1:12 (CEB)

I overheard my neighbours talking as we watched a most beautiful rainbow, its colours brilliant against a thunderous black cloud. 'It's really an optical illusion; it happens when raindrops are angled at 42 degrees to the sun.' 'Which colour is at the top, red or violet?' 'Are there six or seven colours? Indigo doesn't count!' 'What about that pot of gold?'

It was an amusing conversation, but for me it really missed the point. The rainbow, like its creator, is not an object for endless discussion or the hope of affluence, which forever seems elusive. The rainbow is the sign of our Father's promise of his presence and care.

God did not place his covenant bow in the clouds just once; he still fills the skies with rainbows. He is forever renewing his promises. They can clearly be seen in his love tokens day by day: in every kindness and act of forgiveness, in every prayer and every loving touch of faith.

Through a variety of those life experiences I have discovered with eye and heart that the most spectacular rainbows are seen against the darkest skies. The promise of God's presence is always given when we need it most!

Prayer: *Dear Lord, may I never be so immersed in the questions of faith that I miss the signs of your real presence or the touch of your love. Amen*

Thought for the day: Dark clouds are a backcloth for the finest rainbows. Our great hardships may bring great glory to God.

Colin Harbach (England, United Kingdom)

Hope in suffering

Read Lamentations 3:19–26

The steadfast love of the Lord never ceases, his mercies never come to an end.

Lamentations 3:22 (NRSV)

I was devastated when the biopsy showed cancer in my left breast. I felt the weight of the world crashing down on me. I could not stop crying. What will I do? Who will take on my work responsibilities? Where will I get the money for the expensive treatment? In my mind I was questioning God, 'Why me?'

But God showed me that nothing is impossible. Slowly, financial help poured in, and tremendous prayer support came from all over. My loving husband never left my side and nurtured me throughout the difficult period of chemotherapy and recovery. I had a competent and compassionate oncologist. Above all, God encouraged me every day without fail through the Bible and devotional readings.

Six years have passed, and my doctor has announced that I am now cancer-free. Through my diagnosis, treatment and recovery, I came to know for myself that God indeed never fails. God's promises are true. As I enter into retirement, I am excited to discover new avenues for service and to tell my story to inspire others.

Prayer: *God who heals, help us to express our gratitude to you by offering our lives to you for your purposes. Use us for your glory. Amen*

Thought for the day: I will share my story of God's faithfulness with someone today.

Bezalie Bautista Uc-Kung (Quezon City, Philippines)

Worth the effort

Read Psalm 145:13–21

The Lord is near to all who call on him, to all who call on him in truth.
Psalm 145:18 (NRSV)

When I was younger, prayer seemed like a chore to check off my to-do list. I would schedule time to pray and say the words I thought I should. Often I would simply ask for things I wanted, and if I didn't get them I would complain to God.

As I matured in my faith and grew closer to God, I began to ask for less and share with God more, and I often left my prayer time relieved of my burdens and fears. I found that prayer could be surprisingly refreshing – especially if I didn't talk *at* God but spoke *to* God.

Now that I'm older, I've realised that far from being a chore, prayer can be like spending time with a beloved friend. The need to say something is often less important than simply being together. I try to listen more than I talk, and I revel in the joy of being with God.

God will listen to and answer our prayers any time, regardless of what we've done in the past or where we are in our spiritual journey. All we have to do is show up, tune out distractions and open our hearts. I'm not always successful in listening to God, but I've learned that it's always worth the effort.

Prayer: *Dear God, thank you for always being with us. Help us to remember that your love for us is constant and steadfast. Amen*

Thought for the day: I can experience God's love through prayer.

Abigail Gary (Pennsylvania, US)

Patient witness

Read Luke 13:6–9

Let us not become weary in doing good, for at the proper time we will reap a harvest if we do not give up.

Galatians 6:9 (NIV)

As a pastor, I rarely saw significant impact from my sermons, confirmation classes, home and hospital visits, radio and television broadcasts, committee meetings or any other work.

But Jesus' parable of the fruitless fig tree in Luke 13 teaches us that we were created to be fruitful and that we should be patient and graceful towards others. Like the vineyard worker who proposed giving the fig tree more time to produce, we are called to be patient and persistent witnesses and disciples.

We may not see results at first. Someone I taught years ago recently told me that as a youth she did not fully understand or appreciate my lessons, but she reread the class materials as an adult and found new meaning in them. This interaction reminded me that God will use our efforts in time.

The apostle Paul understood this when he said, 'I planted the seed, Apollos watered it, but God has been making it grow' (1 Corinthians 3:6). We are called to be faithful and to trust that God's Holy Spirit, working through many, will bring a good outcome. Let us not grow weary in doing God's work.

Prayer: *We thank you, God, for the gift of salvation and the call to be witnesses in word and deed. We pray in the power of our Savior's name. Amen*

Thought for the day: I can trust God to use my faithful witness for good.

Elmer A. Dickson (Florida, US)

Opportunity to share

Read Romans 10:1–15

How, then, can they call on the one they have not believed in? And how can they believe in the one of whom they have not heard? And how can they hear without someone preaching to them?
Romans 10:14 (NIV)

I am an extrovert, but I find it intimidating to talk openly about Christ and following him. I feel at a loss for words, nervous of how my message will be received and worried that I won't have answers to tough questions. Most people I know who openly speak of Christian faith can easily quote Bible verses for any occasion, have read mountains of Christian literature and never seem to stumble answering any question. That is not me. I feel unprepared and too new in my own faith to tell others about following Jesus.

But then I felt a prompting to 'just start talking'. That nudge quickly became one I could not ignore. I prayed for guidance and courage, and God answered with today's quoted verse. I realised that the Lord knows we will never have all the answers. Yet we still are directed to spread the message of God's love.

Over the weeks that followed, I spoke with many of my non-Christian friends about my faith. Most of my friends listened, a few asked questions and one came to church with me. The more I talked about Jesus, the easier it became. I just needed to listen and follow God's guidance.

Prayer: *Dear Lord, give us opportunities to tell others about your greatness and love. Amen*

Thought for the day: I don't have to have all the answers to share God's love with others.

Jennifer Brigandi (Ontario, Canada)

An invitation

Read Psalm 16:5–11

Now in Christ Jesus you who once were far off have been brought near by the blood of Christ.

Ephesians 2:13 (NRSV)

One day when I was sitting at my kitchen table, I bent down to pick up a dropped utensil. I noticed a single, tiny ant wandering aimlessly on my ceramic tile floor. It was moving around in erratic circles, each growing larger and larger until the ant happened upon a grout line. The ant then continued along the grout line, following it to the door that led outside. Its tiny body slipped under the door, and it crossed the threshold into the freedom of fresh air.

The ant's meandering course made me think about my life's path. As a young man I wandered aimlessly through life; I always felt trapped and without direction. It wasn't until my future wife invited me to church that my life changed. That invitation set me on a path to the freedom found only in Christ. I felt calm as I sensed that I was, at last, headed in the right direction. In time, I crossed the threshold to the fresh air of peace, hope and joy. What a blessing it was to have been shown that path!

Prayer: *God of grace and mercy, thank you for giving us a way to you. Amen*

Thought for the day: My simple invitation can change someone's life of faith.

Thomas Jones (Florida, US)

God's wonderful gift

Read Ecclesiastes 3:1–12

Teach us to count our days that we may gain a wise heart.

Psalm 90:12 (NRSV)

'Let me finish typing this page,' or, 'I'll come as soon as I make one quick phone call.' As a busy pastor, I often said such things to my husband. People had expectations of me, and my responsibilities were a priority. But the page became three pages or the quick phone call lasted an hour, and the ball game was over or the sunset gone before I joined him.

My thinking sounded logical, and it was easy to justify my excuses. Someday, I rationalised, we would have time for each other. My husband never complained, but I was missing golden opportunities with the one I loved. I did not know our time together would be cut short by his fatal stroke at the age of 65.

Today's reading reminds us that there is a time for everything, and in Paul's charge to Timothy, we are told God provides everything for our enjoyment (1 Timothy 6:17). Time with a spouse is meant for enjoyment, but we get caught up in an overabundance of responsibilities that keep us from enjoying the life God wants us to have. In the gospel of Mark, Jesus makes it clear that time with those he loved was important (Mark 6:30–32).

My feeble excuses stole the joy of God's precious gift of time with my husband. Though our work is important, God wants us to be happy in our daily lives.

Prayer: *Dear God, help us not to let responsibilities rob us of time spent with those we love. In Jesus' name. Amen*

Thought for the day: Today I will make the most of God's gift of time.

Jeannine Brenner (Pennsylvania, US)

PRAYER FOCUS: TO APPRECIATE TIME WITH LOVED ONES

Goodness and mercy

Read Romans 8:18–31

We know that all things work together for good for those who love God, who are called according to his purpose.
Romans 8:28 (NRSV)

For 11 years I worked in the province of Huambo, Angola, as pastor and superintendent for a group of churches in my area. In 2017, I was appointed to the province of Luanda, and this change created some inconveniences for my family. My children needed to transfer from their current schools to ones closer to our new home. With the help of some brothers in Christ, we were able to get transfers for two children. It was not easy to find a third transfer.

One morning in my prayer time I was worried. My son said, 'Daddy, have faith; God did not forget us.' God heard my prayer, and later that day we found a third school transfer opportunity.

My son gave me a lesson in faith and hope. When we are with God and believe in God's goodness and mercy, we can wait without worrying. As today's quoted verse reminds us, 'All things work together for good for those who love God.'

Prayer: *Beloved God, teach us to trust in you and to stand firm with faith and hope. We pray in Jesus' name. Amen*

Thought for the day: Trusting in God helps me to wait faithfully.

Mateus Francisco (Luanda, Angola)

Our strength

Read Psalm 91:9–16

I will say of the Lord, 'He is my refuge and my fortress, my God, in whom I trust.'

Psalm 91:2 (NIV)

Backpacking in the Grand Canyon was a dream come true. After weeks of training, I had arrived and was revelling in the beauty. On the fifth and last day, when our group was making the long 4,340-foot climb out to the canyon's South Rim, I felt my stamina waning. Somehow I lost my footing, fell and started rolling uncontrollably down an incline on the canyon wall. A sense of panic swept through me. All the training I had done for the trip and my years of backpacking experience were not enough to break my fall. I could not save myself. Then suddenly, a small bush broke my fall.

This experience reminded me of our human condition. We tend to think that we are self-sufficient. We complete an education, work hard in our profession and plan for retirement, and we often think we have things under control. But when difficulties come into our lives, we are reminded how helpless we are without Christ. Romans 5:6 says, 'You see, at just the right time, when we were still powerless, Christ died for the ungodly.' Our salvation and the strength for our daily lives come from God.

Prayer: *Dear Lord, thank you for being with us each day. Remind us to rely on your strength in our life's journey. Amen*

Thought for the day: When I fall, God is my strength.

Karen McBee (Texas, US)

God's support

Read Isaiah 43:1–7

When you pass through the waters, I will be with you; and when you pass through the rivers, they will not sweep over you.

Isaiah 43:2 (NIV)

An overwhelming number of commitments and a weighty course load left me physically and spiritually exhausted at the end of the college semester. To make matters worse, the weather seemed to mirror my feelings; it had rained for an entire week.

The evening before my last two exams, the rain subsided for a few minutes. I walked hurriedly from the library to my apartment, hoping to avoid the bitter cold and the impending onslaught of yet another storm. My lack of rest amplified my anxiety, and I knew that I needed calm. So while I walked, I prayed for rest and peace.

As I neared my apartment, I paused on a footbridge. Usually the stream flowing under the bridge was quite small, but the recent rains had forced it beyond its banks. As water crashed over the rocks that usually kept it contained, I remembered today's quoted verse: 'When you pass through the rivers, they will not sweep over you.'

When I feel overwhelmed, I remember the overflowing stream and know that I am not like the its submerged rocks. In the most stressful moments, God will not let my trials sweep over me. Instead God will provide calm, strength and guidance.

Prayer: *Dear God, when we are overwhelmed, remind us of the calm, strength and counsel that faith in you provides. Amen*

Thought for the day: Regardless of what weighs me down, I know that the Lord is with me.

Samuel Driggers (Georgia, US)

In the moment

Read Luke 5:1–11

Jesus sat down and taught the crowds from the boat.

Luke 5:3 (CEB)

Recently a friend told me of his plan to travel to the other side of Australia to see the wildflowers. I told him of my experiences in the Fitzgerald River National Park, which is renowned for its spectacular wildflowers. Although it was well past the official wildflower season when I visited, I was overwhelmed by the beauty and variety of flowers still blooming. Talking with my friend brought back some of the joy I had experienced. It put me back in the moment.

I am glad that the gospel writers put together vibrant and meaningful stories that capture much of what it was like to be with Jesus and to hear what he had to say. Their stories of what Jesus said and did can put us back in the moment. From the time that I was a small child, I have enjoyed hearing the stories of Jesus because we get a sense of what it would have been like to be there.

Being able to imagine what Jesus meant to the people of that time is a precious gift scripture gives us. It helps us to grow in our faith and understanding.

Prayer: *Loving Father, thank you for the stories of Jesus' life and teachings. Thank you for the people who have shared those stories with us. Amen*

Thought for the day: What story from scripture can I experience anew today?

Meg Mangan (New South Wales, Australia)

Promises in uncertainty

Read Psalm 36:5–9

How priceless is your unfailing love, O God! People take refuge in the shadow of your wings.

Psalm 36:7 (NIV)

When the future seems uncertain and I don't know what I can hold on to and trust, I find it helpful to remind myself of three of God's promises from scripture.

First, God's love is constant. Our jobs, status and relationships can change in a moment. But when life gets hard or we mess up, God is there showing us limitless and unfailing love.

Second, God's protection is certain. Psalm 36:7 reminds us that God is our shelter and refuge. No matter the storm, God will protect us and faithfully remain by our side. We can always hold on to God.

Third, we can count on God's provision. Jesus tells us that we don't have to worry, because our heavenly Father knows our needs and will provide for us (Matthew 6:31–33). For me, God's physical and spiritual provision have always been there.

Though life might not always be great, God is faithful to God's promises. Amid changing circumstances, we can hold on to these promises from our unchanging God.

Prayer: *Dear God, thank you for your promises to us. Help us to hold on to your faithful presence when we face uncertainty. Amen*

Thought for the day: Even in my uncertainty, God is faithful.

Adam Weber (South Dakota, US)

 PRAYER FOCUS: SOMEONE EXPERIENCING BIG CHANGES

Entertaining angels

Read Deuteronomy 10:17–22

You shall also love the stranger, for you were strangers in the land of Egypt.

Deuteronomy 10:19 (NRSV)

My husband and I invited Mina and her husband over for coffee and dessert. They are from Iran and had moved to our small town for graduate studies seven months earlier. But they told us that we were the only people in our town who had befriended them so far.

As I read a thank-you note from Mina, I remembered the summer I spent in Taiwan on a volunteer trip. I didn't speak the language, the food was unfamiliar, the customs were new to me and I looked different from everyone else. But through the hospitality of strangers, I was able to adjust and enjoy myself. That experience made me more aware of how international students, immigrants, refugees, asylum seekers and other newcomers may feel. I know firsthand how refreshing it is when a stranger shows care, tries to get to know you or introduces you to their loved ones.

We can all relate in some way to being an outsider. The Israelites were foreigners in Egypt, Jesus was an outsider in Jerusalem and as Christians our home here is only temporary; our eternal home is in heaven. We can always demonstrate love and compassion. As Hebrews 13:2 instructs, 'Do not neglect to show hospitality to strangers, for by doing that some have entertained angels without knowing it.'

Prayer: *Gracious God, help us to always show kindness and compassion to strangers and to be your hands and feet in the world. Amen*

Thought for the day: Today I will show hospitality to strangers.

Rebecca Bolin (Texas, US)

PRAYER FOCUS: PEOPLE WHO ARE NEW TO MY TOWN

Choose joy

Read Genesis 12:1–9

The Lord said, 'Do not be afraid, Abram. I am your shield, your very great reward.'

Genesis 15:1 (NIV)

I often think about Abram/Abraham, and his story inspires faithfulness and obedience in me. I relate to his story, because my own life story is similar in several ways.

Abram was not young when God called him to migrate from the land of his family, and neither was I. He was 75; I was 58. Abram went from material wealth to material wealth. But God told me, 'I have something better for you than material wealth. My plan for you is spiritual wealth, living as a poor person in rural Honduras.' God changed Abram's name to Abraham (see Genesis 17:5). And I also changed my name to better serve God.

I have read Abraham's story over and over. It never says how he felt about leaving his home. But I am encouraged that I have the same freedom. I get to choose whether I walk through my new life with joy or with reluctance and bitterness. Most of the time, I am able to choose joy, but sometimes I still become discouraged. Being called by God is not a guarantee against discouragement. But even when we become discouraged, we can find a deep joy in faithfulness and satisfaction that we are following God's call for our lives.

Prayer: *Dear God, help us to savour the joy of faithfulness and obedience. Thank you for being our shield and our great reward. Amen*

Thought for the day: I can choose how I feel about following God's call for me.

Sister Alegría del Señor (Colón, Honduras)

A living example

Read Ephesians 4:11–16

Speaking the truth in love, we will grow to become in every respect the mature body of him who is the head, that is, Christ.

Ephesians 4:15 (NIV)

After I gave a short orientation speech to the parents of our preschool class, three-year-old Miriam told her mother that she liked 'the sermon'. Miriam's father is the pastor of the church where our preschool is located. Along with teaching the normal preschool curriculum, I read Bible stories to the kids and pray with them before snack-time each day. These faith-filled actions have become part of our daily routine.

With a loud and sometimes chaotic class of 20 preschoolers, I have wondered just how much of my teaching they retain. Also, I have often felt that I just wasn't doing enough in the church to serve God. However, after reflecting on Miriam's words, I realised that my actions and prayers are a way to teach the youngest in our church about Jesus. I am serving God in the little things I do every day. By being an example for my students, I am teaching them about faith and following Jesus. I may not be delivering a sermon, but my actions can be a living example of faith. We all can serve God through our words and actions of love – to children and adults alike.

Prayer: *Creator God, help us grow in our faith as we become living examples of your love. In Jesus' name. Amen*

Thought for the day: I can serve God through my daily activities.

Christine Roger (Illinois, US)

Seeking approval

Read John 10:22–30

My sheep listen to my voice; I know them, and they follow me.
John 10:27 (NIV)

As my wife and I prepared for a visit from our new in-laws, we noticed things around the house that hadn't bothered us before. The dinner plates seemed old, the hardwood floors squeaked and the windows weren't clean enough. We felt certain these small imperfections would be detected by our guests. Even our rose garden, which we lovingly maintained, became something to worry about.

As I sat and stared at a bunch of white, yellow and red roses – wondering how I was going to get everything done – it occurred to me how my life seemed to revolve too much around the opinions of others. The need for approval from colleagues, friends and family members seemed to occupy most of my thoughts, which left little room to hear from God. I permitted the words of people to drown out God's word. But God doesn't want us bound by the opinions and criticism of those around us. Rather, as children of God, we are to seek God's approval and God's thoughts.

God's opinion should matter most. Other people's views may seem a reliable way to measure successes and failures; but in truth, only God's opinion is trustworthy. Only God can set us free from the hold that others' opinions may have on us.

Prayer: *Dear God, help us to hear your voice over the many voices that divert our attention from you. Amen*

Thought for the day: God's opinion of me is what counts.

Doug Lim (California, US)

Lions and bears

Read 1 Samuel 17:19–37

'The Lord, who saved me from the paw of the lion and from the paw of the bear, will save me from the hand of this Philistine.'

1 Samuel 17:37 (NRSV)

For three years I faced one challenge after another. I was diagnosed with burn out and depression, and I had to give up my profession as a teacher. Since then, I have had to deal not only with my recovery, but I have also struggled to pay the rent, other bills and even to buy groceries. However, God has taken care of my husband and me every time.

After each moment of uncertainty, I realised how much more I trusted God. Through each of these trials, I saw God strengthening our faith for the next challenge. We learned to be confident in God and God's promises for our lives.

I think David might have felt the same way when he faced Goliath in the valley of Elah. Although he was a youth and an unseasoned soldier, God had been strengthening and training him as he tended his father's sheep. God helped David protect the flock from the attack of lions or bears, and David learned to trust God. On the day of battle, David was confident in God's ability to grant him victory against the Philistine champion.

With this lesson in mind, we can trust in God's plan as we face our own lions and bears.

Prayer: *Wonderful God, thank you for strengthening our faith in times of adversity. Help us to fulfil your purposes for our lives. Amen*

Thought for the day: God can use my adversities to strengthen my faith.

Madeline Twooney (North Rhine-Westphalia, Germany)

A powerful light

Read John 12:44–46

Then God said, 'Let there be light'; and there was light. And God saw that the light was good; and God separated the light from the darkness.

Genesis 1:3–4 (NRSV)

While walking to an evening worship service, I saw the soft, warm light from the sanctuary's stained-glass windows glowing in the night. The windows provided a welcome but limited illumination to my surroundings. It occurred to me that this outward-bound light pales in comparison to what we experience during daytime services, when the sunlight pours through the windows and fills the church with brilliant colour and warmth.

Sunlight is a symbol of the light that God gives to us – how vital and powerful both are for our lives. Just as the brightness of daylight far outshines the light that comes from the church windows at night, God's light is infinitely more powerful than what we humans can produce. Yet this humbling comparison can encourage us to continue with our outreach efforts, so that God's light can shine through us, illuminating the loving message of God for all people everywhere.

Prayer: *Dear God, help us to recognise our limitations, even as we seek to share the gospel with others. As Jesus taught us, we pray, 'Our Father in heaven, hallowed be your name, your kingdom come, your will be done on earth as it is in heaven. Give us today our daily bread. And forgive us our debts, as we also have forgiven our debtors. And lead us not into temptation, but deliver us from the evil one.'* Amen*

Thought for the day: God's light is infinitely bright.

Wayne Brent (Texas, US)

 PRAYER FOCUS: THOSE WHO TRAVEL FAR TO ATTEND CHURCH

*Matthew 6:9–13 (NIV)

God's comfort

Read 2 Corinthians 1:3–11

The Lord is close to the broken-hearted and saves those who are crushed in spirit.

Psalm 34:18 (NIV)

'I have difficult news for you,' said the doctor. 'You have cancer.' Shock and fear washed over me. Then came heartbreak and tears. Thus began the endless rounds of scans, medical appointments and chemotherapy treatments. Battling cancer has been the toughest journey of my life. But God has held me firmly as we walk along this rocky path together, and along the way I have experienced God's peace and healing.

One day, as I was sitting in the cancer centre's packed waiting room, I took a moment to study the faces of those around me. I saw fear, worry and discouragement. I knew how they were feeling, because I felt it too.

I heard God's clear call to comfort these fellow suffering souls. So I became a volunteer driver with an organisation that coordinates free transportation for cancer patients to life-saving treatments and medical appointments. As I ride along with my new friends, we may discuss our latest treatment or procedure. Or we may just chat about a favourite restaurant or the weather. And sometimes we say nothing at all, because there are no words. But most importantly, I have many opportunities to show God's compassion and to share Jesus' message of love and hope in ways I could never have imagined.

Prayer: *Loving God, keep us aware of those around us who are hurting. Help us comfort them as you have comforted us. Amen*

Thought for the day: God's compassion can speak without words.

Molly Johnson (North Carolina, US)

God's voice

Read 1 Kings 19:9–14

If you fully obey the Lord your God and carefully follow all his commands that I give you today, the Lord your God will set you high above all the nations on earth.

Deuteronomy 28:1 (NIV)

Our home is located next to a park where I often walk with my young daughter in the early spring. When the birds begin their spring migration, the park is filled with birds and their singing. One day we heard an exceptionally pleasant song, but we couldn't locate the bird. I asked my daughter to be quiet, and we both listened carefully. After some time of patient listening, we saw a little grey bird that was producing the beautiful sound. We had to remain quiet in order to hear the voice of the bird.

Later that night, I started to think about stories in scripture that relate to that experience. Sometimes we complain that we cannot hear the Lord's guiding voice. But we may not hear it because our minds can be filled with so many other thoughts. In those times, we can use the same method my daughter and I used to hear the bird. We can put aside all unnecessary things, remain quiet in prayer and focus only on God.

Prayer: *Dear Lord, help us to quiet the chaos in our minds so that we can take the time to hear your voice, accept it and put into practice what you tell us. Amen*

Thought for the day: I can hear God's voice if I listen for it patiently.

Dmitri Semjonov (Rakvere, Estonia)

 PRAYER FOCUS: SOMEONE SEEKING GOD'S GUIDANCE

Is it enough?

Read John 6:5–13

Andrew… spoke up, 'Here is a boy with five small barley loaves and two small fish, but how far will they go among so many?'

John 6:8–9 (NIV)

I used to be a speech therapist in a Christian hospital in Hong Kong. One time, an old man with a stroke came in repeatedly, making an unintelligible request with increasing desperation. He was waiting to see a consultant, so I thought he had got muddled. Finally he drew out a piece of paper that said 'Cannot speak'. I then understood that, although he was waiting for another clinic, he had seen the sign on my door and was asking for speech therapy. I promised to do what I could, but after he had gone I put my head on the desk in despair. I had no more therapy time to see him, he lived over an hour away by bus and his name suggested he spoke a dialect I was not familiar with.

With little hope, I asked our social worker if she could help. She found out that the old man had been befriended by a young man in his block of flats, and this young man was willing to carry out therapy plans if I could write them. It also turned out my Chinese assistant spoke the old man's dialect. He was brought regularly for therapy by his young friend and he improved enough to go out for meals with his friends.

In today's passage it seems the resources were not available to meet the people's need. In Jesus' hands, however, five small loaves and two fish are enough to feed thousands of people, with plenty left over. If we bring the little we have to Jesus, he can take it, bless it and give it out in a way that multiplies it, way beyond our expectations.

Prayer: *Lord Jesus, take the little I have to give you today and multiply it for your kingdom.*

Thought for the day: In Jesus' hands, what we have is enough.

Gillian Tettmar (England, United Kingdom)

PRAYER FOCUS: THOSE WHO FEEL THEY HAVE NOTHING TO GIVE

Patience

Read Psalm 130:1–5

I wait for the Lord, my soul waits, and in his word I hope.

Psalm 130:5 (NRSV)

I recently began a new hobby – candlemaking. In my first class, I made a candle by layering different shades of blue. I had to wait for the first layer to set before pouring another. The waiting process taught me patience.

Being patient is a vital part of life. Throughout our life of faith, we may wait to see the answer to our prayers. Patience with God and our circumstances is one sign of a mature faith, a quality that we develop over time.

In the Bible, God answered many prayers only after much time had passed. Jacob waited seven years for a wife and worked seven more after being cheated by his father-in-law (Genesis 29:15–30). The Israelites waited four decades for deliverance (see Exodus 16:35).

We wait for what is worth waiting for; in the process, we learn patience. May God grant us patience to wait for God's divine blessings.

Prayer: *Father God, grant us patience to keep anticipating, hoping and trusting in you as we wait. In Jesus' name we pray. Amen*

Thought for the day: Patience helps my faith mature.

Mary Ng Shwu Ling (Singapore)

Love others as yourself

Read Matthew 22:34–40

This is the first and greatest commandment. And the second is like it: 'Love your neighbour as yourself.'
Matthew 22:38–39 (NIV)

One of my friends in high school suffered from depression and suicidal thoughts. I tried to reassure my friend that I would always be there for support and encouragement, which my friend appreciated. But despite all the actions that I – and others – took, my friend died by suicide.

For a long time I couldn't see God in that situation. I felt responsible for my friend's death, and it damaged my self-worth. I felt like I wasn't enough. But then friends in my Bible study reminded me of the second greatest commandment according to Jesus: 'Love your neighbour as yourself.' If I couldn't forgive and love myself, then that guilt and anger would hinder my efforts to love others.

It's difficult to forgive and relearn how to love effectively, but those things are necessary for a life with others and a life with Christ. I continue to work on loving myself while I strive to love others as Jesus commanded.

Prayer: *Dear God, thank you for the everlasting love and mercy you show us. Give us the strength to love ourselves and others like you love us. Amen*

Thought for the day: God loves me, and I can love myself too.

Sam Engle (Kentucky, US)

Powerful words

Read 2 Timothy 3:10–17

It is the spirit that gives life; the flesh is useless. The words that I have spoken to you are spirit and life.

John 6:63 (NRSV)

I was confident that I was going to get an A in my humanities course. I had earned nearly perfect grades and eagerly participated in classroom discussions throughout the semester. Now it was time to reap the benefits of my labour. But instead I reaped bewilderment when my instructor showed me my final grade: C.

I asked my instructor for an explanation, and he began to read aloud the syllabus that he had handed out on the first day of class. He read that a student who arrives late to class would be counted as absent, and a certain number of absences would penalise his or her final grade. I realised that I had arrived late to class several times, and that was why I received a C, despite my hard work.

Although it was disappointing, that experience led me to carefully read every syllabus for the rest of my college career. I've since graduated from college, but today I still try to read important words with great care. And the words found in the Bible are immeasurably more powerful than those found on any syllabus. The Bible contains God's message for us to read, believe and apply. Without fail, it will provide positive direction for our lives.

Prayer: *Dear God, renew our minds daily with your word through the power of your Holy Spirit, so that we will live worthy lives. Amen*

Thought for the day: God's word gives direction to my life.

Aaron Caruso (Connecticut, US)

God is good

Read Psalm 145:1–9

The Lord is good to all, and his compassion is over all that he has made.

Psalm 145:9 (NRSV)

When I went through a difficult time, it was hard for me to understand what God was doing in my life. Everyone else seemed happy except me. I asked many questions: Why won't God answer my prayers? Why do others have their heart's desires when I am living for God? Why doesn't God love me? What have others done for God that God has been so good to them?

I started to believe that God did not love me, and I became frustrated and depressed. It took me many years to recognise God's goodness in my life and all the ways that God has blessed me.

I began to see that while things were not going the way I wanted them to go, God was still working for good. Finally I began to trust in God and understand that God shows goodness to each of us in different ways.

We may not understand why bad things happen to us or why God does not give us the things we ask for and think we need. When we question God's goodness, we can pause to think of all our blessings. This practice can help us realise that God has been good to us and will continue to be.

Prayer: *Dear God, open our eyes to see your goodness to us. In Jesus' name. Amen*

Thought for the day: God desires good things for my life.

Enid Adah Nyinomujuni (Dar es Salaam, Tanzania)

Being present

Read John 5:1–18

When Jesus saw him lying there, knowing that he had already been there a long time, he asked him, 'Do you want to get well?'
John 5:6 (CEB)

Each Saturday morning a men's group from the church where I am a pastor meets for breakfast at a local restaurant. It's an opportunity for men to talk honestly about their faith and the issues they face.

I enjoy these gatherings, but at times my mind is everywhere except the group's conversations. I get concerned that people can't hear one another, I worry that new people in the group may feel left out and I often watch the restaurant staff, hoping they don't mind that we're lingering and taking up a few tables. My focus on why we're gathering – faith formation and relationship development – gets lost.

In scripture we see that Jesus was focused and knew that God was present in all situations. The phrases 'Jesus saw' and 'Jesus looked' appear dozens of times in the Bible. And in today's reading, Jesus was surrounded by people and noise and yet was able to truly see one man. Nothing else mattered to Jesus except that interaction.

So many things distract us from focusing on the present moment. Let us learn from Jesus not to miss the opportunities that God places before us every hour of every day.

Prayer: *Creator God, help us to slow down, focus on what's in front of us and experience your love here and now. Amen*

Thought for the day: The present moment holds abundant holiness.

Christian Coon (Illinois, US)

 PRAYER FOCUS: LEADERS OVERWHELMED BY RESPONSIBILITIES

None forgotten

Read Luke 10:25–37

A Samaritan, who was on a journey, came to where the man was. But when he saw him, he was moved with compassion.

Luke 10:33 (CEB)

It has often intrigued me that Jesus commended a social outcast in his parable about the good Samaritan. But until recently, I hadn't paid attention to the fact that of the ten lepers Jesus healed, the only one to return and thank Jesus for healing him was also a Samaritan (Luke 17:11–19). And the woman at the well to whom Jesus revealed himself as the Messiah was a Samaritan too (John 4:3–42).

At one time I acutely felt on the outside of society, labelled and misunderstood. I saw no way to become more connected to it. But Jesus Christ reached out and healed me. His living water quenched my thirst in body, mind and soul. And he brought people into my life to whom I could be of service, which restored my dignity and allowed me to feel needed. Jesus always sees our true worth and lifts us up to that level.

Jesus not only accepts those the world ignores; he often gives them special recognition and attention. No matter our status or circumstance, none of us is forgotten by Jesus.

Prayer: *Dear Lord, thank you for helping us when we feel forgotten by others. Help us to see our true worth. Amen*

Thought for the day: No one is an outcast in Jesus' eyes.

Victoria Walsh (Montana, US)

PRAYER FOCUS: THOSE WHO FEEL EXCLUDED

Stronger than fear

Read John 20:24–29

Now faith is confidence in what we hope for and assurance about what we do not see.
Hebrews 11:1 (NIV)

One day at church, I came across this saying: 'Faith is stronger than fear.' This reminded me of a difficult situation when my family and I found this to be true.

Our daughter Rebeca called us one day to tell us that her four-year-old son, Esteban, had been hospitalised because his liver enzymes were dangerously elevated. He became a candidate for a liver transplant. Of course we felt great fear, but at the same time, with our united strength, we were able to say that with God nothing is impossible. Our whole family was grounded in the certainty and conviction that God would work a miracle in our grandson.

We placed our complete faith in God to face our great fear, and God sustained us. We rejoiced and gave thanks to God when Esteban made a full recovery.

Prayer: *Merciful God, continue to sustain us by your grace as we pray, 'Our Father which art in heaven, Hallowed be thy name. Thy kingdom come, Thy will be done in earth, as it is in heaven. Give us this day our daily bread. And forgive us our debts, as we forgive our debtors. And lead us not into temptation, but deliver us from evil: For thine is the kingdom, and the power, and the glory, forever.'* Amen*

Thought for the day: When I despair, God will help me overcome my fears.

Vidal Cruz Rosado (Puerto Rico)

 PRAYER FOCUS: CHILDREN WAITING FOR AN ORGAN TRANSPLANT

*Matthew 6:9–13 (NIV)

Power to provide

Read Philippians 4:10–19

My God shall supply all your need according to his riches in glory by Christ Jesus.

Philippians 4:19 (KJV)

It was a cold, snowy winter. My three children and I were down to crackers and ketchup in our cupboard. My husband had moved out and was not providing food for the household. One evening in prayer I told God that we had nothing to eat. Then I got my children bathed and ready for dinner, trusting and believing in God's power to provide. Before I had finished setting the table, there came a knock at the door. A friend from my church had brought several bags of groceries for us.

My friend mentioned that our local grocery store had a 'buy one, get two free' sale. She had brought the 'free' items to us and added even more. She said, 'The Holy Spirit instructed me to bring this to you.' Overwhelmed with joy, I thanked God for meeting our need.

The blessing did not end there. My sister in Christ prepared a full meal, with dessert, for my family and hers. We were blessed with dinner and wonderful company. That experience reminded me of the truth that God can provide for our needs. My cupboards and my heart were full.

Prayer: *Gracious God, send your Holy Spirit to those who are suffering and help us to meet every need according to your riches in glory by Christ Jesus. Amen*

Thought for the day: How can I answer the prayer of a neighbour today?

Kellie Heisler (New Jersey, US)

Planting seeds

Read 1 Corinthians 3:6–9

I planted the seed, Apollos watered it, but God has been making it grow.

1 Corinthians 3:6 (NIV)

I love working in my garden. I am amazed that tiny seeds planted in the soil can sprout and grow into large plants that produce tasty vegetables and beautiful flowers. The vegetables become part of my meals, and the flowers brighten the day. Each time I work in my garden, I remember God's wisdom in creating tiny seeds that will become tomatoes, beans, cucumbers or peas. I work to prepare the soil and make sure I have a sunny spot to plant. Then I plant the seeds and water them when necessary. But I cannot make the plant grow; only God can bring growth from those tiny seeds.

In our spiritual life, we can plant seeds of faith in others by sharing what God has done for us – by doing a work of love in Jesus' name or by sharing the good news of the gospel. We cannot finish the work of bringing others to Christ, just as we cannot make seeds grow and flourish in a garden. But we are co-labourers with God in planting and watering.

Prayer: *Our Father, may we plant the seeds of love that you will bring to fruition. In Jesus' name we pray. Amen*

Thought for the day: How will I plant a seed of God's love today?

Verner Guthrie (Alabama, US)

A simple reminder

Read Psalm 92:1–4

I can do all this through [the Lord] who gives me strength.
Philippians 4:13 (NIV)

I was feeling the stress building up at work, and I wasn't handling it very well. It wasn't possible to walk away from the situation, so instead I took a few moments to restart my computer. When the login box appeared, I typed in my username. Then I paused and smiled in the middle of a secular workroom as I typed in my password, which reminded me how much Jesus loves me and needs me to be right where I am.

My work password has to include at least eight characters in a combination of upper- and lowercase letters, numbers and a symbol. I had previously realised that the Bible provides perfect variety for this: book name, chapter number, colon and verse number. Every morning I start my day with a reminder that God is at the heart of everything I do. When I lose sight of God's presence at work, I restart my computer and have the opportunity to reaffirm that God is with me.

Every month I get to pick a new affirmation to start my day. I take my time over this decision. I even look forward to changing my password! I enjoy this simple way of incorporating God into my digital life.

Prayer: *Dear Lord, help us to keep you at the centre of our lives so that we will remember to call on you in all circumstances. Amen*

Thought for the day: In what simple ways can I remind myself of God's presence?

Lorna MacIntyre (Scotland, United Kingdom)

Rich inheritance

Read Ephesians 1:3–12

By grace you have been saved through faith, and this is not your own doing; it is the gift of God.

Ephesians 2:8 (NRSV)

Upon achieving the senior rank of chief petty officer in the navy, I adopted this saying: 'Never forget where you came from.'

As a young adult I walked away from the faith that had been modelled for me by loving Christian parents. I forgot where I came from, even though the inheritance was freely given through my Lord and Saviour.

Years later, on a navy warship in the middle of the ocean, I found myself broken and bitter. At that moment I remembered where I came from. I remembered the sounds of my father praying in the middle of the night – calling out family members' names (including my own) in the name of Jesus. I repented and rededicated myself to Jesus Christ, and I vowed to make sure that I modelled my faith, prayed for others and encouraged my sons and everyone around me in the rich heritage of a faithful Christian walk as it had been passed on to me.

Prayer: *Heavenly Father, help us to remember your great love for us when we forget where we came from. Help us to lift up those who are struggling with their faith and to call out their names to you as others have done for us. Amen*

Thought for the day: I can model faith for others as it has been modelled for me.

Steven A. Schofield (Virginia, US)

From sticks to blossoms

Read 1 Kings 19:1–5

We wait in hope for the Lord; he is our help and our shield.

Psalm 33:20 (NIV)

For much of the year, bushes known as desert broom appear to be a mass of bare, green sticks. During its dormant period, a broom bush may go unnoticed. When its twigs are cut in even lengths, tied together and attached to a long wooden handle, they can be used as a household tool to sweep debris. In spring, buds appear on the bush and then burst forth into bright yellow blossoms. Their glorious fragrance summons passersby to inhale their lovely scent. Doing so makes those long months seem worth the wait.

When I pass by bare broom bushes in winter, I remember that Abraham and Sarah waited years for God to fulfil the promise of a son. David, the shepherd, must also have felt the difficulty of waiting between the time of Samuel's anointing of him and his eventual crowning as king.

Then, like blossoms on the broom bush, the waiting was rewarded: Isaac was born to Abraham and Sarah; David was crowned king, first of Judah and then also of Israel.

As we wait through seemingly barren times, we can remember the lesson of the broom bush. The bare, green sticks of our lives can blossom, making the wait worth it.

Prayer: *Dear Lord, help us to remember the blossoms of the past as we wait for those to come. Amen*

Thought for the day: I will wait expectantly for what God has in store for me.

Mary Hunt Webb (New Mexico, US)

PRAYER FOCUS: SOMEONE EXPERIENCING A BARREN TIME

Used cans

Read Luke 8:26–39

Jesus sent him away, saying, 'Return home and tell how much God has done for you.'

Luke 8:38–39 (NIV)

Years ago, I knew a little girl who collected used cans on the street. She liked to write on scraps of paper and put them in the cans. Most people in the street ignored her, and she was often insulted and called 'used-cans girl'. What she did was considered stupid and meaningless.

When she grew up, she remembered that she had been invited to church when she was young. She felt the Holy Spirit encouraging her to go to church, so she went. There she heard the story of a man who was an outcast – unclothed, living in a cemetery, possessed by demons and considered insane. Yet Jesus helped him, and God's love saved and changed the man. No one is meaningless for Jesus.

In the same way, even when people did not respect the girl and considered her worthless, Jesus sought her, loved her and changed her life. The 'used-cans girl' is now used by God to teach, write, build mission houses and preach the great love of God. That little girl was me. Even when we feel worthless, like used tin cans – thrown away and trampled on, we can shine the light of Jesus for God's glory.

Prayer: *Dear Jesus, thank you for your amazing and saving love. Remind us that through you we are worthy and can shine light for your glory. Amen.*

Thought for the day: Jesus loves me even when I feel unworthy.

Linda Chandra (Banten, Indonesia)

Love grows

Read Leviticus 19:9–18

When you reap the harvest of your land, do not reap to the very edges of your field or gather the gleanings of your harvest… Leave them for the poor and the foreigner.

Leviticus 19:9–10 (NIV)

Our church college group has been transformed through acts of service to residents and transients in our city. We were studying the book of Leviticus, and we were discussing the practice of leaving the gleanings (a portion of the harvest) as an act of loving our neighbour. One woman asked, 'Why just the gleanings? Why not more?' Since we live in an urban setting nowhere near a farm, we created our own garden and named it Harvest of Hope. Seeds grew along with our love for our community.

We came up with the idea of a 'reverse tithe'. We kept the gleanings and gave away most of the produce. On our first distribution day, the woman who originally posed the 'why not' question handed a box of produce to someone and said, 'I am so glad to meet you; we grew this for you.' Her comment reflected her joyful obedience to God's command to love our neighbour. For the college group, it was the gift of love that kept on growing!

Prayer: *Gracious God, we praise you for providing what we need. Help us to be aware and active in serving those in need with the resources you have so graciously given to us. Amen*

Thought for the day: How is God leading me to share what I have with others?

Mike Medeiros (California, US)

Not alone

Read Daniel 3:13–30

May you be made strong… and may you be prepared to endure everything with patience, while joyfully giving thanks to the Father, who has enabled you to share in the inheritance of the saints in the light.

Colossians 1:11–12 (NRSV)

After a night at the children's hospital with our daughter, I did not welcome the telephone ringing at 7.00 am. I saw that the call was from my oldest son, Barry, who had been in another hospital for a few days with the flu. Irritated by the early hour, I answered the phone sleepily – but it wasn't Barry on the phone. It was a nurse calling to tell me that Barry had died.

Barry was a diabetic and in renal failure, but he had recently made great strides in taking care of himself. Set to graduate from college after working at it for 17 years, his sudden death seemed particularly cruel in light of his recent progress. Grief, compounded by concern for our daughter, threatened to overcome me.

Our pastor pointed out in a sermon that though God didn't take Shadrach, Meshach and Abednego out of the fire, God did protect them. I finally understood that God does not promise freedom from difficulties. In fact, Jesus specifically said that his followers would have 'distress' (John 16:33, CEB). But God promises to be with us through whatever we face.

Whenever grief wells up, I draw strength from knowing that God is here with me and will work things together for good (Romans 8:28).

Prayer: *Loving Father, thank you for your presence with us in our challenges. Help us draw strength from you. In Jesus' name we pray. Amen*

Thought for the day: God will be with me through any difficulty.

Donnell King (Tennessee, US)

What a blessing!

Read Psalm 19:7–11

[Jesus] went up on a mountainside by himself to pray.
Matthew 14:23 (NIV)

When my parents became Christians, they spent time reading the Bible and praying daily. My father gave me my first copy of *The Upper Room* when I was 13; my mother, now 95, continues to use this devotional guide each day.

I am grateful for my parents' example of regularly spending time with God's word. Over the years, I have tried to make spending purposeful time with God a priority each day. Time spent studying scripture not only leads to a better understanding of who God is and God's purposes but also builds faith, brings joy and creates hope.

The Upper Room has been a part of my devotional time throughout my life. I have been blessed many times by meditations or Bible readings for the day that were just what I needed. I am always amazed by God's timing and love for me when it feels like God is speaking to me personally through the devotional.

What a blessing it is to build the disciplines of prayer and Bible study into each day! What an encouragement to be part of a praying community of believers from diverse countries and cultures!

Prayer: *Loving Father, thank you for the blessings that come from setting aside time to read your word and to pray each day. Amen*

Thought for the day: Time spent in God's word is always worthwhile.

Ann Stewart (South Australia, Australia)

No excuses

Read Luke 14:15–24

Another said, 'I have bought five yoke of oxen, and I am going to try them out; please accept my apologies.'
Luke 14:19 (NRSV)

When I was eight years old, my teacher told me I was a gifted writer. That was the first time someone had told me I was good at something. As a teenager I wrote in a journal occasionally, while dreaming of being published. But each time I felt a nudge from God to write something meaningful, I found other things to do – distractions that kept me from doing what God wanted. By the time I finished high school, I had convinced myself that no one would read what I wrote. For decades, I gave God a lot of excuses. Yet through prayer and support, I made a decision this year to follow God's leading.

In Luke's gospel, Jesus tells a story about a great dinner party. One by one invitees give reasons why they cannot attend. One has a field to tend, while another has animals to care for. Haven't we all given God similar excuses? Someone may love to cook, yet avoids volunteering at a shelter. People skilled in business or technology decline to help with a church project that requires those skills. Imagine all that can be accomplished if we stop making excuses! When we give all that we are, we create a world that is closer to resembling what God desires for us.

Prayer: *Eternal Father, forgive us for making excuses. Continue to guide our path so that we may serve you more wholeheartedly. In Jesus' name, we pray. Amen*

Thought for the day: Sharing our gifts by serving others creates a better world.

Kelly Desclos-Estes (Virginia, US)

Heavenly parent

Read Matthew 7:7–11

[God] comforts us in all our trouble so that we can comfort other people who are in every kind of trouble.

2 Corinthians 1:4 (CEB)

Being a parent doesn't come with a job description or manual. It is on-the-job training all the way. As a father, I am always learning. I am no superhero or mighty pillar of strength. I am only a parent. When my child hurts, I react. When my child cries out, I hear. When my child asks for help, I do what I can to help.

So why don't I let my heavenly Father do for me what I am more than willing to do for my own children? Why do I try to do it all myself? I am finally learning to go to my heavenly Father when I am frightened, lonely, bruised or hurt.

God reassures us: 'The Lord your God is with you, the Mighty Warrior who saves. He will take great delight in you; in his love he will no longer rebuke you, but will rejoice over you with singing' (Zephaniah 3:17, NIV). I'm learning that God is waiting to give me comfort as a parent who wants the best for me, a father who will pick me up and hold me in his arms. God our Father won't go away – ever!

Prayer: *Teach us, O Lord, to trust in your unfailing love. Amen*

Thought for the day: I can allow God to be a father to me.

Michael Morelan (Alabama, US)

A closer look

Read Matthew 25:31–46

Bear ye one another's burdens, and so fulfil the law of Christ.
Galatians 6:2 (KJV)

Twice a year my church picks up trash along two miles of roadway. We divide into groups and start at each end, working until we meet each other.

I remember the first time we went out. I was scanning the sides of the roads while riding to our starting point. Upon our arrival, I said, 'This shouldn't take long; there's not much trash along this section.' We gathered up our bags and equipment and started out. About two minutes into picking up trash, I changed my mind. What I could not see riding by at 25 mph, I could see now that I was slowly walking. Where did all these pieces of plastic, foam, paper and glass come from?

It then occurred to me that this same problem of perspective applies to other aspects of my life. How many people do I come in contact with each day at church, at the store, the bank or at work, only to say, 'How are you' and barely wait to hear the response, 'Fine and you?' If I'm so busy with my own life that I quickly pass others by, I may be missing an opportunity to bear someone else's burden. It could be as simple as a word of encouragement, a listening ear or a prayer. When I slow down enough to hear or see the struggle in another's life, I can 'fulfill the law of Christ'.

Prayer: *Heavenly Father, help us to see those around us who need lifting up. In Jesus' name, we pray. Amen*

Thought for the day: If I slow down, God can show me opportunities to lift others up.

George Hilliard (Virginia, US)

 PRAYER FOCUS: ROADSIDE CLEANUP CREWS

The costly perfume

Read John 12:1–8

Mary took about half a litre of pure nard, an expensive perfume; she poured it on Jesus' feet and wiped his feet with her hair.
John 12:3 (NIV)

Mary made her way to Jesus, poured costly perfume on his feet and wiped his feet with her hair. The house was filled with the fragrance. The perfume was worth about a year's salary for a skilled labourer. She expressed the depth of her love and devotion to Jesus with an extravagant gift. Others misunderstood her act, but Jesus accepted it. He honoured her gift and told those around him to leave her alone. According to Mark's gospel, Jesus told the others that her sacrifice would be remembered forever (Mark 14:9).

Mary wasn't bothered by others' opinions or comments. Showing her thankfulness for Jesus – who had accepted, loved and valued her – mattered most. Mary showed us that the best form of worship is the one that most genuinely represents our love for God.

In the same way, we can pour out the praises of our hearts. We surrender our lives fully to Jesus through sacrifice and service. When we pour out our hearts to give fully of ourselves to Jesus, the fragrance of our love and devotion will fill our surroundings.

Prayer: *Dear God, help us pour out our hearts to you and offer you our praise. Amen*

Thought for the day: What gift can I offer Jesus today?

Elizabeth Livingston (Maharashtra, India)

Joy amid grief

Read Psalm 139:7–12

Call to me and I will answer you, and will tell you great and hidden things that you have not known.
Jeremiah 33:3 (NRSV)

In the months following my mother's death from ALS, I started my first semester of college, began a new job and painfully continued life without my mum here to be a part of it. As unbearable as life without her can seem, I still somehow manage to find moments of joy that the Lord offers me in my grief.

Jeremiah 33:3 was my mum's favorite verse. Throughout her life, I never saw her doubt that the Lord was with her. When her final days were coming, I know she was filled with peace and joy because she knew in just a matter of time she would see her Saviour. She called out and God answered her – daily. She didn't know exactly what God was doing amid her suffering – only that God was present and would never abandon her.

Even on days when my grief seems unbearable, I remember that God walked through the ALS with my mum, walked with me as I witnessed her life ending and still walks with me today. I sometimes struggle to be joyful and to live in the present. But the Lord is right here next to me – sustaining me through it all.

Prayer: *Dear Lord, give us the strength to overcome whatever trials we face. We place our lives always in your hands. Amen*

Thought for the day: Joy is found in the Lord.

Kristen Phipps (Texas, US)

Hope of new life

Read Matthew 6:25–34

There is hope for a tree, if it is cut down, that it will sprout again, and that its shoots will not cease.

Job 14:7 (NRSV)

I had returned from the city of Natal, where I had spent seven long years with my family. I was almost 50 years old and was starting over after a failed professional experience. The prospects were not promising. As I was praying about my situation, I noticed that a large tree in the complex where I lived was extremely dry. Sometimes branches fell, putting at risk those who happened to be passing underneath. I saw no hope for that tree and thought it should be cut down.

Spring came, and one morning I went to the balcony to look at the tree again. It was leafy and beautiful, with a huge green canopy! At that moment, I felt God speaking to my heart: 'I will do with your life just as I did with this tree.' My heart was filled with laughter, hope and trust in God.

Today, I am a renewed and successful professional. I was reborn after a period of drought. God brought a miracle into my life that turned my story of failure into victory, to the glory of God. God is faithful, immensely good, and delights in the well-being of his children.

Prayer: *Unchanging God, help those hearts that are dried up by the failures and hardships of life to find the hope of new life in you. Amen*

Thought for the day: God can make everything new in my life.

Alexandre de Azevedo (Rio de Janeiro, Brazil)

PRAYER FOCUS: FOR NEW PROFESSIONAL OPPORTUNITIES

Open ears

Read Proverbs 2:1–10

The Lord gives wisdom; from his mouth come knowledge and understanding.

Proverbs 2:6 (NRSV)

The other night my young daughter was talking on the phone with her cousin. As she got ready to get off the phone, she said to him, 'I'm about to get off of here; is there anything else you want to tell me first?' I have thought often about her way of ending her call – it struck me as a rather unique way to end a conversation.

As I thought more about it, I realised how wise I would be to follow my daughter's approach – not necessarily on my phone calls but during my prayer time. What if before ending my prayers, I asked God, 'Is there anything else you want to tell me?'

Sometimes I am guilty of forgetting to stop and listen to what God may be trying to say to me when I pray. What if, instead of just 'hanging up' on God, I stopped to listen to what God might have to say first? Instead of my doing all the talking, I want to learn to give God plenty of time to speak to me. From now on, I am going to see what God has to say before I 'hang up'.

Prayer: *Father God, open our ears so that we can hear what you want to tell us each day. Amen*

Thought for the day: When I pray, I will listen as much as I speak.

Katrina Douglas (Tennessee, US)

Job

A year will have passed between the time that I write this and when you read it. We work on each issue of the magazine far in advance to allow time for translation and distribution around the world. This poses a unique challenge in responding to current or recent events because by the time the issue goes to press those events will be neither current nor particularly recent. So I tend to avoid references to events that are occurring as I am writing. However, given the past couple of weeks, both in my own community and in the world, I feel deeply compelled to break with this tradition.

On the night of 2 March and in the early morning hours of 3 March 2020, tornadoes killed several people and destroyed even more homes and businesses in Middle Tennessee. As we have struggled with the tragedy and loss caused by the storms, we are also dealing with the uncertainty and anxiety of the Covid-19 pandemic and mourn the havoc that it is wreaking at home and across the globe. I feel the weariness of my neighbours; and I feel my own.

As I try to make sense of it all, my mind keeps turning to Job and his story. Job is likely not the first person to whom we would think to look when reaching for a word of hope. Job offers, however, one of the finest examples we have of what it looks like to persevere in the face of seemingly insurmountable adversity. In the first two chapters of the book, Job faces unimaginable loss – his property, his family, even his character is called into question. How could anyone in Job's position carry on?

We often attribute patience to Job as the primary virtue that distinguishes him from other characters in scripture, but were you to ask me, I would say that higher on that list are his persistence and tenacity in questioning God and God's presence in his circumstances. Chapter after chapter Job argues with God and demands answers concerning his plight.

I see more of myself in Job than anyone else in the Bible – not so much the side of Job that was resilient and somehow remained steady in the face of unthinkable tragedy and loss, but the part of Job that was relentless in his questions and need to understand. Job wanted to know how God could allow everything that had happened to him and wondered where God was in the aftermath. And I don't blame him. I am with Job on that. 'Today... my complaint is bitter,' Job says. 'O that I knew where I might find [God]!' (Job 23:2–3, NRSV).

Job's story reminds me that there is something deep within human nature that searches out meaning and understanding in our suffering and loss. But like the events of the past few days, Job's story ultimately leaves me with more questions than it does answers. God says to Job, 'Where were you when I laid the earth's foundation?... while the morning stars sang together and all the angels shouted for joy?' (Job 38:4, 7, NIV). God seems to be saying to Job that even were God to explain it, Job couldn't possibly understand. In one sense, I have never found this response all that satisfactory or helpful. But in another, I find it inexplicably beautiful. Maybe it's the image of the stars singing or angels shouting with joy. I can almost let myself hear it as God's way of saying to Job that there might not be as much to understand or as much meaning to be found in hard times as we would want. Sometimes it is just bad – plain and simple. But God is still God.

If there is a word of hope in Job, it is not in how the story ends. Hope comes long before God restores Job's life. 'I know that my redeemer lives,' Job says, 'and that in the end he will stand on the earth' (19:25). Here Job recognises that God is in the business of redemption and can bring good from the bleakest circumstances. I am always struck that Job doesn't speak these words after his struggle is over – he utters them in the middle of it! That in itself is enough to give me the persistence and hope to imagine that while there are hard days ahead and though life might not have completely returned to normal by the time you read this, evidence of God's work of redemption in our lives and the lives of those we love will most certainly surround us.

Andrew Garland Breeden
Acquisitions editor

Faith not fear

Read Jeremiah 29:10–14

Be strong and courageous. Do not be afraid; do not be discouraged, for the Lord your God will be with you wherever you go.
Joshua 1:9 (NIV)

Making decisions can be tough – especially life-altering ones. When I chose my college, I made the safest decision possible. Friends, finances and proximity to family were my considerations, all of which were designed to help me play things safe. Twenty years later, when I was choosing a seminary, those same concerns emerged. Then, I heard this question: What decision will require you to trust God the most?

Walking by faith and not by sight is seldom easy. Security seems to be one of our most basic priorities. If only we understood that we can never secure our lives and futures on our own. Imagine what would happen if we trusted God's words from Jeremiah 29:11: 'I know the plans I have for you… plans to give you hope and a future.'

God's love for us is truly greater than our fears and insecurities. Every day we get new opportunities to make decisions not rooted in our fears but grounded in God's love.

Prayer: *Dear Lord, you know the plans you have for us. We ask you to move us towards them in faithful confidence. Amen*

Thought for the day: Today I will decide by faith, not by fear.

Eleanor L. Colvin (Texas, US)

PRAYER FOCUS: PEOPLE FACED WITH HARD DECISIONS

Carried

Read Psalm 46:1–7

The Lord himself goes before you and will be with you; he will never leave you nor forsake you. Do not be afraid; do not be discouraged.
Deuteronomy 31:8 (NIV)

When I was eight years old, I fell on a broken bottle; the glass cut my knee to the bone. The doctors stitched up my wound and wrapped my leg from my hip to below my knee. Every night my dad had to carry me up the stairs to bed. The first morning when he carried me back down, I looked at the bottom of the stairs and grabbed his neck tightly. Dad said, 'I've got you.' The fear let go, and so did I. I don't remember the trips up or down for the next six weeks.

Before I accepted Christ into my life, I was living with the same sense of panic I felt that first time my dad carried me down the stairs. I was wounded and figuratively immobile. There seemed no way for me to simply rest – no place to be at peace. But when God called to me, 'Do not be afraid,' my sense of relief was profound. I let go, and God has carried me ever since.

Prayer: *Loving God, thank you for carrying and holding us. When we have fallen, when we are broken, when we can no longer move, you call, 'Do not be afraid.' In every situation of our lives help us to rest in you. Amen*

Thought for the day: Through all the ups and downs of my life, God says, 'I've got you.'

Steven Scheid (Tennessee, US)

Something new

Read John 15:9–17

Jesus said, 'As the Father loved me, I too have loved you. Remain in my love.'

John 15:9 (CEB)

When I was in primary school, I remember several children talking about having to give up candy for Lent – and not being at all happy about it. But we don't just have to give up things we enjoy for Lent. We can also give up bad habits like putting ourselves down, thinking badly of others, gossiping or having unrealistic expectations of ourselves. These habits restrict love, rather than help it grow. And who knows, when we give up negative thoughts, words or behaviours for Lent, we may find that we enjoy it so much that we wish to give them up forever.

But Lent is not just for letting go of things; it can also be about taking something up. After all, Jesus took up his cross. Perhaps we could take up reading more about Christ during Lent, trying new ways of praying or take more time to enjoy simply being in God's presence. Maybe we could choose to reach out to someone we don't know well.

God can lead us in all sorts of ways. Instead of feeling resentful about giving something up for Lent, we may find ourselves looking forward with anticipation to the new experiences God is calling us to in this season.

Prayer: *Living Lord, guide and challenge us during Lent. Help us to discover anew your grace and love in this season. Amen*

Thought for the day: Letting go of bad habits can free me to experience God's love.

Meg Mangan (New South Wales, Australia)

The blessing of tears

Read Revelation 21:1–4

You have kept count of my tossings; put my tears in your bottle. Are they not in your record?
Psalm 56:8 (NRSV)

When I think of God's blessings, I think of family, friends, sunshine or even my morning cup of coffee. Until recently, I never considered tears a blessing. For the past three years I have struggled with one son's cancer, another son's diminishing eyesight, and, finally, the loss of my husband of 58 years. Through it all I found I was unable to cry. I kept everything within me – like a heavy weight attached to my ribs. I had always been private with my tears, but now I couldn't cry at all. Finally, after the death of my husband, I have begun to cry. It happens unexpectedly, at odd moments; sometimes just a trickle, sometimes seemingly endless sobs. But whether my tears flow like a stream or a waterfall, they leave me refreshed, with the weight in my chest becoming lighter and my spirit cleansed.

As we walk through life, we often miss blessings hidden in calamities. But while tears can blur our vision, they can also clarify our sight to reveal new truths. Perhaps we can see our way to reach out to someone in pain. I believe that when we have walked through pain and grief, we may be the only ones able to see clearly another person walking the same path – and there our tears can meet. Truly, tears can be God's blessing for this life.

Prayer: *Dear Jesus, because you also wept, you understand our tears. Thank you. Amen*

Thought for the day: God can renew my spirit through my tears.

Eleanor Cowles (Oregon, US)

Choosing community

Read Proverbs 13:16–21

Whoever walks with the wise becomes wise, but the companion of fools suffers harm.

Proverbs 13:20 (NRSV)

When I was in high school, I tried to spend time with people from different friend groups and backgrounds. I spent time with my friends from my church youth group. But I was the captain of my cross-country team and spent a lot of time with my teammates too. When I was around my cross-country friends, I would sometimes catch myself acting differently than I would when I was with my friends from church. My behaviour got to a really bad point during my junior year. In my senior year, the Lord opened my eyes to see that I was not modelling Christlike behaviour.

We need to pay close attention to the people we spend the most time with. When I was spending time with certain people, I was moving away from the Lord. Today's verse says that if we surround ourselves with like-minded believers, then they will support us as we grow towards the Lord.

I know that I cannot go through my Christian walk alone. The book of Acts reminds me that we are called to be in community with other believers. Our lives of faith are richer when we surround ourselves with faithful companions.

Prayer: *Dear God, thank you for friends who draw us closer to you. Amen*

Thought for the day: Christian community can help me grow in my faith.

Austin Shumake (Texas, US)

My hope

Read Psalm 25:4–15

Guide me in your truth and teach me, for you are God my Saviour, and my hope is in you.

Psalm 25:5 (NIV)

The loneliest Christmas I ever spent was when my spouse had to work outside the city, leaving me alone with our baby who was sick at the time. So when my neighbour asked me to watch her 12-year-old daughter because she wanted to go to the hospital, I agreed.

After putting my baby to bed, the girl and I read the story of Jesus' birth. She had never heard about Jesus, but she was interested, so I gave her the book. Her mum picked her up the next day, and I lost touch with them because we moved away.

David also experienced loneliness. But in David's loneliness, he said, 'My hope, Lord, is in you' (Psalm 25:21). As God did for David and for me, God can change loneliness into something valuable.

Seven years later, I met the girl on the train. She told me that she and her mum had since become Christians. After that night when she stayed at my house, her heart wanted to know more about Jesus – she still keeps the book I gave to her. She is now taking theology classes and feels called to be an evangelist. As she spoke, I cried tears of happiness. My heart rejoices because God is in me, and God is my hope.

Prayer: *Dear Father, give us hope when we feel lonely. Show us your ways, O Lord, and teach us to follow you. Amen*

Thought for the day: Even when I feel alone, God is my hope.

Linda Chandra (Banten, Indonesia)

The ancient paths

Read Micah 6:6–8

The Lord proclaims: Stop at the crossroads and look around; ask for the ancient paths. Where is the good way? Then walk in it and find a resting place for yourselves.

Jeremiah 6:16 (CEB)

Ivy climbed the exterior walls of our house and spilled out over a small garden beside our garage. It added character to our home and ground cover to our garden, but I knew it was time to trim it back. After gathering my tools, I knelt in the cool grass to dig up some of the roots, weeds and grass that had crept into the garden. It wasn't long before I hit something hard. Scraping through the black soil, I discovered it was a red brick. I kept scraping and found another and another until I had unearthed a brick walkway lining the garden. I wondered how long that old brick pathway had lain hidden by neglect and overgrowth.

As I scraped soil from the bricks, I thought of Jeremiah. The prophet's people were turning away from God and following their own paths. In response, Jeremiah warned them to stop and seek 'the ancient paths' long hidden by their rebellion against God's ways. Jeremiah called them back to God's ancient paths of justice and faithful devotion.

God's ways may be ancient, but they hold meaning for us today. Those red bricks reminded me that I had been neglecting God's timeless paths. I vowed to walk them again, knowing they would lead me into eternal life with God.

Prayer: *Holy Spirit, call us back to you when we stray from your ancient paths. Help us to walk faithfully with you. Amen*

Thought for the day: What path is God leading me to discover today?

David R. Schultz (Illinois, US)

PRAYER FOCUS: GARDENERS

What now?

Read Isaiah 40:26–31

Those who wait for the Lord shall renew their strength, they shall mount up with wings like eagles, they shall run and not be weary, they shall walk and not faint.

Isaiah 40:31 (NRSV)

A few years ago I retired from ministry after about 40 years, and then four months later my husband died after a long illness. He had also been in ministry for over 40 years. My grief is monumental. As time goes by I ask myself, 'What now?' Day by day I wait for the Lord to lead me. Volunteer opportunities abound, but at this point in my life, my scoliosis limits my physical activities.

One day recently it came to my mind that I have written sermons and articles for years; what about trying to write devotionals? So here I am writing devotionals, hoping to continue a new way of ministry.

Isaiah asks, 'Do you not know? Have you not heard? The Lord is the everlasting God, the Creator of the ends of the earth' (Isaiah 40:28, NIV). Those who faint and grow weary are given power and strength regardless of our age. The prophet reminds us, 'Those who wait for the Lord, shall renew their strength, they shall mount up with wings like eagles, they shall run and not be weary, they shall walk and not faint.'

Prayer: *Dear God, our creator, nourish us as we wait for your leading. In Jesus' name. Amen*

Thought for the day: I can find renewed strength when I wait for the Lord.

Mary Alice Potter (North Carolina, US)

Traces of faith

Read 2 Timothy 1:3–7

Blessed are those who fear the Lord, who find great delight in his commands.

Psalm 112:1 (NIV)

One warm summer day, my mother took my brother and me by the hand and led us into the 'clean room'. In Hungary, until the last century, the clean room was a special part of the home, particularly in village houses. It was considered the nicest room and used only for special occasions or for hosting guests.

That day, we knelt together and prayed in the pleasant coolness of the room. First we listened as Mother prayed. She poured out her fears for our sick father while weaving in the events and feelings of our everyday lives with thanksgiving. Then my brother and I spoke our own prayers.

The clean room in our house showed traces of our faith. We prayed together so much in this room that there were marks in the carpet showing where we knelt. I remember the comfort, peace and good feelings from these times of prayer. The way my mother lived out her deep faith left a strong impression on me; it led me to a loving and caring relationship with Jesus Christ.

In today's scripture reading, the apostle Paul recalls the sincere faith that Timothy's grandmother and mother had passed on. Timothy bore the traces of his family's faith. How good it is to be people of faith and to express our questions and fears with thanksgiving in prayer!

Prayer: *Dear God, thank you for listening to all the thoughts, desires and joys of our hearts. Amen*

Thought for the day: What traces of faith do I leave behind?

Anna Kerekrétiné Szili (Budapest, Hungary)

Healing touch

Read Mark 1:40–45

Moved with pity, Jesus stretched out his hand and touched him.
Mark 1:41 (NRSV)

My mind was reeling over our daughter's premature birth, her birth defects and then having to leave my wife in another hospital. At the neonatal intensive care unit there, I stood watching my baby. She looked so tiny and fragile. Then a nurse said, 'Touch her. She needs your touch.' I hesitated, but the nurse insisted. The notion that the awkward touch of a dazed father could contribute to her healing surprised me. While I gently touched her, I thought of how she needed God's healing touch just the way all of us do at times.

When in profound grief, I have felt God's love in a friend's hand on my shoulder. When other Christians have laid their hands on me in prayer, I have experienced a divine joy and peace I never knew before. Their hands were God's hands for me.

Although we cannot physically feel God's hand as my tiny daughter felt mine, we can experience God's presence as we are healed, comforted, blessed, calmed and transformed through the actions of those who love us.

Prayer: *O God, thank you for surrounding us with your healing love. Amen*

Thought for the day: Our loving actions can be God's presence to others.

Sam Wright (Florida, US)

 PRAYER FOCUS: NEONATAL NURSES

From within

Read Psalm 139:1–18

I am fearfully and wonderfully made.

Psalm 139:14 (NIV)

Psalm 139 has always been my favourite part of the Bible. When I was a child, it taught me that I was special. I felt that I had a unique purpose in life, that there was something only I could do. As I grew up, I didn't think as much about my unique purpose as other things took over.

One day I was in the grocery store with a full cart headed for the checkout queue. Another woman with an equally full cart got there first. I was annoyed. Couldn't she see I was in a hurry? Then I heard a voice in my head: 'She is also fearfully and wonderfully made.' Immediately, I was humbled and realised that was true. Then I heard, 'Pray for her.' *What?* I was still struggling to let go of my irritation, but I said a simple prayer for her.

I have no idea how the rest of her day went, but I noticed a change in myself. After I prayed, I was no longer angry. I felt genuine love for the woman. I realised that God wanted me to pray not just for her but for myself as well.

Prayer transforms us from within. What a wonderful world it would be if we all prayed for one another and allowed our praying to transform our thoughts and actions.

Prayer: *Heavenly Father, help us to remember that each of us is made in your image. Remind us to treat others as your beloved children. Amen*

Thought for the day: Praying for others is good for my soul.

Melody Baggech (Oklahoma, US)

PRAYER FOCUS: SOMEONE WHO ANNOYS ME

A forever love

Read Romans 8:35–39

Who will separate us from Christ's love?
Romans 8:35 (CEB)

I once read a newspaper article that said a significant number of young people want to find a love that will last forever. However, finding a love that lasts can be a challenge.

The hymn writer George Matheson (1842–1906) was rapidly going blind at age 19. He had fallen in love with a girl at school, and they planned to marry. When he told her about his condition, he asked if she would still marry him. She said no.

On the evening of his sister's wedding, recalling his own pain and lost relationship, Matheson wrote his famous hymn 'O love that wilt not let me go'. In it he wrote, 'I give thee back the life I owe, that in thine ocean depths its flow may richer, fuller be.' The words of the hymn refer not to human love but the immense love of God, from which nothing can separate us. Some loves are reciprocated; others are not. But we can always count on the enduring love of God, a love that will never let us go.

Prayer: *Eternal God, thank you for first loving us. Create in us loving hearts and spirits as we pray, 'Father, hallowed be your name, your kingdom come. Give us each day our daily bread. Forgive us our sins, for we also forgive everyone who sins against us. And lead us not into temptation.'* Amen*

Thought for the day: God's love will never let me go.

Hugo N. Urcola (Buenos Aires, Argentina)

 PRAYER FOCUS: PEOPLE WITH IMPAIRED VISION

*Luke 11:2–4 (NIV)

Only a pinch

Read Luke 13:18–21

To what should I compare the kingdom of God? It is like yeast that a woman took and mixed in with three measures of flour until all of it was leavened.

Luke 13:20–21 (NRSV)

The last time my two grandsons and I made pizzas, I tried a new recipe for the dough. I watched as a tiny packet of yeast, activated by a little warm water and a bit of sugar, helped to create a bowl of rapidly expanding dough.

The power of that yeast is like that of the tiny clove of garlic I added to my pizza sauce. It was a small amount in proportion to the large can of tomato sauce, but as the pizza warmed in the oven, the flavourful aroma of that tiny clove of garlic began to fill the room.

Scripture tells us that the kingdom of God is like a mustard seed or a small pinch of yeast – or a clove of garlic. The impact our faith has on others may start out small, but it can grow into something significant. Just as a seed or yeast dough or the aroma of garlic grow to their full potential under the right conditions, the kingdom of God grows by every tiny contribution of faith and trust.

When we worry that others have more to offer God or that we have nothing of significance to offer, we can remember the tiny pinch of yeast or a mustard seed. God can create the right conditions for our faith to have a positive influence on those around us.

Prayer: *Compassionate God, help us remember that even our small acts of faith and service to you will grow under the right conditions. Amen*

Thought for the day: God can use my small acts of faith to have a big impact.

Beverly Marshall-Goodell (Georgia, US)

PRAYER FOCUS: GRANDPARENTS AND GRANDCHILDREN

God delivers us

Read Psalm 27

The Lord is the strength of my life; of whom shall I be afraid?… Though an host should encamp against me, my heart shall not fear: though war should rise against me, in this will I be confident.

Psalm 27:1, 3 (KJV)

El Salvador had been in a civil war for nearly a decade when, in November 1989, those who sought to overthrow the government brought the fight to the capital city, San Salvador, where I lived. For a few days, my family and I were trapped in our house, hiding from gunfire from airplanes, helicopters and the armies fighting right outside.

I was only nine years old at the time, and I knew nothing of the politics and the violent events that escalated into this awful conflict. But I was afraid and felt that all hope was lost. I began to cry. My mother came to me and asked me, 'Why are you crying?' I said, 'We are going to die.' I'll never forget her response: 'Where is your faith? Trust the Lord.' Her words brought me confidence, and I felt better. It was a few days before we could safely escape our home. The night after we left the city, I saw formations of helicopters hovering and firing red flares over the area where we had lived.

It is not easy to have faith when your life is in danger or you can see no solution. Nevertheless, the Bible tells of many people who trusted God to deliver them from danger. God has not changed. Every time I remember this event from my childhood, I thank God for delivering me and my family so that I could grow in faith and share my faith with others.

Prayer: *Dear God, deliver us from danger and from those who would do us harm, for you are our refuge and our saviour. We trust in you. Amen*

Thought for the day: God is powerful to deliver me from danger.

Marcelo Carcach (Maryland, US)

Keep the faith

Read John 18:33–38

Blessed are they that mourn: for they shall be comforted.
Matthew 5:4 (KJV)

I was raised in a Christian family, but I did not cultivate the habits of daily prayer or church attendance during my childhood.

After age 20, I began to embrace habits like praying, reading the Bible and other religious books, and reflecting with others on the Christian life. At that time I also learned the importance of serving, tithing and contributing to church work. As I deepened my reading of scripture, I strengthened my faith, became closer to God and improved my character.

However, I have been unable to advance my career. I feel I have been repeatedly passed over for promotions and misunderstood. But in spite of this, I have not lost my faith or the habits of praying, doing good to others and fulfilling God's will. Thanks to these practices, I have been able to endure all these difficulties. When we face challenges, we can be strengthened by the love and mercy of our faithful God.

Prayer: *Dear God, help us to endure tribulations and keep our faith firm in you. We pray in the name of Jesus. Amen*

Thought for the day: I can endure difficulties because of my unshakable faith in God.

Anabela Couto de Castro Valente (Luanda, Angola)

Strength

Read Psalm 61:1–3

Hear my cry, O God; attend unto my prayer.
Psalm 61:1 (KJV)

One day while I was getting ready to go to work, my dad called. He told me that my mum had passed away in her sleep. My heart sank. I called my boss and told him I would not be in that day. Then I made the five-minute drive down to the beach. When I got there it was so foggy that I could see only about 25 or 30 feet into the ocean. I thought to myself, 'This is exactly how I feel right now. What is next? What do I do? What do I pray? I can't do this.'

I had no answers. As I looked out into the fog, I dropped to my knees and tearily called out the first three verses of Psalm 61. Suddenly I heard a seagull squawk. When I looked up, I still could not see anything but fog, but somehow I finally felt peace begin to wash over me. I got up, walked back to my truck and drove home repeating Psalm 61:1–3.

It has not been easy learning to live without my mum. I still miss her every day. My wife, dad, sisters and church family are all around me; they have helped carry me through. Most important, God has given me the strength I need. And when I don't know what to pray, I pray the Psalms.

Prayer: *Heavenly Father, thank you for being with us in all circumstances. In Jesus' name we pray. Amen*

Thought for the day: God can give me strength when I need it most.

George Hilliard (Virginia, US)

God can relate

Read Matthew 4:1–11

The devil left [Jesus], and angels came and took care of him.

Matthew 4:11 (CEB)

For several years I taught third grade in the same classroom where I had attended third grade. On the first day of school each year, I would pass around my third-grade class picture and inform my students that I had once sat at one of the small desks, drunk from the little classroom water fountain and gained knowledge from things written on the old chalkboard. I found it especially helpful when attempting to put students new to our school at ease. I let them know that I could relate to their feelings of anxiety, apprehension and excitement because I had been 'the new kid' in the same classroom.

As Christians, we worship a Saviour who can relate to our needs and emotions. I find great comfort in knowing that Jesus understands the human joys and trials we experience.

God sent Jesus to live among us and to set an example for our lives. By reading and studying the Bible, we know Jesus has firsthand knowledge of temptation, hunger, loneliness, disappointment, grief, rejection and physical pain as well as love, peace, joy, kindness and contentment. We serve an awesome God full of compassion for us.

Prayer: *Dear Lord, how wonderful it is to know that you not only recognise but can relate to our human needs! Help us to convey your empathy and compassion to others. Amen*

Thought for the day: I will look for ways to show empathy and compassion today.

Sally Hassler (Indiana, US)

What's the plan?

Read Exodus 13:17–22

By day the Lord went ahead of them in a pillar of cloud to guide them on their way and by night in a pillar of fire to give them light, so that they could travel by day or night.

Exodus 13:21 (NIV)

After graduating from high school I had plenty of choices and different ideas about the shape my life could take, but I had no clear vision for my future. I had to find answers to many questions. We are sometimes tempted to make our own plans and set goals for the future without considering God's plans for our lives. So I decided to continue my studies by attending seminary and to search for God's guidance.

In Exodus, God ordered Moses to lead the people out of Egypt. Moses had no clear map, development plan or carefully designed strategy for the journey to the promised land. All he could do was to trust in God.

As we search for God's plans for our lives, we can trust that God will fulfill those plans. Even in the most difficult situations when our human perspectives offer no good solutions, we can rely on God to show us the way.

Prayer: *Dear God, help us to trust in you and to have faith that the best plans are the ones you lay before us each step of our life's journey. Amen*

Thought for the day: I can trust that God knows my situation.

Naatan Hollman (Tallinn, Estonia)

Treasures

Read Matthew 6:19–21

Store up for yourselves treasures in heaven.
Matthew 6:20 (NIV)

My family and I emigrated from India to the United States in the early 1980s. Just like that, bags were packed and goodbyes were said as my parents, two sisters and I headed to our new country. Being from a faithful Christian family, we knew it was essential that we pack the family Bible to take with us.

During those first months in our tiny Brooklyn apartment, I remember our nightly custom of my father reading from the Gujarati Bible and then praying together as a family.

Recently I came across the family Bible, and I noticed that it had fallen apart. The leather cover had peeled off and the dried-up binding could not hold the pages together. The physical book did not withstand the test of time, but the living word of God is eternal. Physical things, objects and humans deteriorate with time. In the timeless words of the Bible, God gives us renewal and freshness and promises us the gift of eternal life. If we keep God's words in our heart, they will never fade. Therein lies the true treasure.

Prayer: *Eternal God, thank you for showing us that while treasures on earth fade with time, treasures in heaven will last an eternity. Amen*

Thought for the day: The Bible is the living word of God.

Shital Sherri Macwan (New York, US)

Letting go

Read Ephesians 4:29–32

Get rid of all bitterness, rage and anger, brawling and slander, along with every form of malice.

Ephesians 4:31 (NIV)

When I was 13 years old, I entered my pet Charolais calf in the local county fair. I had raised the calf from the time he was born. He was so white and fluffy I had named him Cotton.

When it was time to show Cotton, I led him into the arena. Halfway into the show ring something startled him, and he bolted. I held on to the lead strap, and he dragged me across the sawdust floor. The show ring helpers were yelling, 'Let go! Let go!' When I finally did let go, I had some scrapes and a bruised ego.

Too often we hang on to negative attitudes, feelings and behaviours which can cause harm to ourselves and to others. Bitterness, rage and anger are just some of the feelings that cause damage as we focus only on ourselves. If we act on these feelings, they can hurt others as well. Most important, negative behaviours can hinder our Christian witness. Such harmful attitudes hold us back from being loving, forgiving persons.

When we become angry or hurt, we can listen as the Holy Spirit urges us to 'Let go!' Then, with the Spirit's help, we can rid ourselves of the attitudes, feelings and behaviours so harmful to ourselves and others and become who God calls us to be.

Prayer: *Heavenly Father, help us to listen to the Holy Spirit telling us to let go of harmful attitudes and behaviours so that our speech and actions may be pleasing to you. Amen*

Thought for the day: What attitudes or feelings is God inviting me to let go of?

Sandi Ann Lumpkin (Indiana, US)

Read the manual

Read Psalm 119:89–104

Your word is a lamp to my feet and a light to my path.

Psalm 119:105 (NRSV)

The grouting should not have been a difficult job, but the result was not satisfactory. I realised I'd made my usual mistake: I hadn't read the instructions.

I'm the same with everything. When I assemble furniture, I survey the finished items and find they are not perfect. There are pieces back to front or upside down, or the drawers stick. I'm especially prone to not reading the manual for my car. I fumble for the instructions at the side of the road when I need the fog lights, wonder how to adjust the side mirrors or need to change the clock twice a year. The answers are all in the book that I forget to study.

The most important manual I've ever read and then forgotten to apply is the Bible. God has given us a book that can help us figure out how to live. While it does not offer direct help for every situation, the Bible includes guidelines that can equip us for living a God-filled life.

If stuck on the bookcase shelf and ignored, the Bible is about as useful as my neglected car manual. In every situation, the Bible can guide us.

Prayer: *Dear Lord, thank you for the Bible. Encourage us as we read it, and guide us as we apply it to our lives. Amen*

Thought for the day: What can I learn from the Bible today?

Carol Purves (England, United Kingdom)

The master architect

Read Matthew 7:24–27

In their hearts humans plan their course, but the Lord establishes their steps.

Proverbs 16:9 (NIV)

When I was growing up, I longed to know how my life would play out. Maybe I would be a professional footballer or a successful business owner. But during my mid-teens, my life took a drastic turn, and I was sent to prison. I thought my life was ruined, and I felt hopeless. Sitting in my cell, I replayed my life as if it were a movie. I looked at every scene from every angle. After much evaluation, I came to understand that everything I had chased after was meaningless.

One day in that lonely cell God called to me. From that moment on, my life took a turn for the better. I felt that God was building my life on a solid foundation. Even now, God is continuing to create something new in me. And when I think of the years past, I can see the master architect at work. God has been directing my steps, one at a time.

When our lives seem aimless and purposeless, we can learn to trust God, the creator and sustainer of life. When we trust God's directions, we can be assured that God will lead us to a life of goodness and purpose.

Prayer: *Dear God, guide our steps so that we can build your kingdom. Amen*

Thought for the day: God is the foundation of my life.

Antonio Delapaz (Texas, US)

Mosaic

Read 2 Corinthians 4:7–12

We know that in all things God works for the good of those who love him, who have been called according to his purpose.

Romans 8:28 (NIV)

While driving home from a trip, I encountered a spectacular scene at a rest area. From the outside, the building appeared to be a plain brick building. However, when I opened the door, I saw a beautiful mosaic celebrating the state of Missouri that filled an entire wall. I gasped in awe as I saw ornate scenes of butterflies landing on brilliantly coloured flowers, steamboats on the swirling river and images of people who made an impact in the state. When I stepped closer to try to get a better view, I saw the broken pieces of pottery and glass that were carefully placed in cement to create this beautiful picture.

The mosaic reminded me that God can use the broken pieces of our lives to create a beautiful story. When I give God my broken pieces – heartache from losing a job, pain from a failed relationship, suffering from a serious illness – God can mould me to become more like Christ. I can trust God to work for me even when I do not see how the brokenness in my life will turn out for good.

As the broken pieces of pottery created a beautiful story, God can use our brokenness to give others hope. Together we can tell a beautiful story of God's restorative love.

Prayer: *Heavenly Father, we give you the broken pieces of ourselves. Help us to trust that you will restore us and create something beautiful from our brokenness. Amen*

Thought for the day: I can trust God with the broken pieces of my life.

Heather Hagstrom (Kansas, US)

PRAYER FOCUS: ARTISANS

Like never before

Read Acts 3:1–10

Taking [the lame man] by the right hand, [Peter] helped him up, and instantly the man's feet and ankles became strong. He jumped to his feet and began to walk.

Acts 3:7–8 (NIV)

I often think my family's situation will never change. We will never have our own home, our brother will never recover from mental illness and we will never be free from our financial difficulties. One day a friend said to me, 'Lina, you should pray like never before.' I thought, 'What does he mean "like never before"? Should I begin praying with my eyes open rather than shut? Should I pray standing rather than sitting?' Later I came to understand that 'like never before' means I should pray with full trust in God. Rather than looking at my family situation as something that will never change, I should look to God, who has the power to change everything.

'Like never before' reminded me of the lame man at the temple gate, thinking he would never be able to walk, much less jump. Then one day he met Peter and John. Instead of giving the man money, Peter said, 'In the name of Jesus Christ of Nazareth, walk.' Immediately the man 'jumped to his feet and began to walk'.

The power of God and the faith and witness of Christ-followers like Peter and John can assure me that when I face a situation that I think will never change, I can pray 'like never before' and put full faith in God, whose power can change everything.

Prayer: *Almighty God, in difficult situations help us to trust that you can do miracles like we have never seen or heard of before. Amen*

Thought for the day: Today I will put my trust in God's power.

Linawati Santoso (East Java, Indonesia)

Acts of kindness

Read Galatians 6:7–10

Let us not become weary in doing good, for at the proper time we will reap a harvest if we do not give up.

Galatians 6:9 (NIV)

My wife enjoys working in her colourful flower garden, which adds beauty to our yard. But she also works full-time, spends many hours with a local charity, is a Girl Scout troop leader and takes care of our family. With so much going on, her flower garden needed some work. She came home one day and said that she was going to give up her flowers; she didn't have the time to maintain them properly.

I don't have a green thumb, but I woke up early the next morning, grabbed my gloves and portable radio, and went to work on the flower garden. As I cleared out the weeds, I listened to praise music and thanked God that I had the health, ability and opportunity to do the work. I also praised God for my wife, who does so much for our family and others. It only took a few hours, and it didn't really feel like work. That one act of kindness brought happiness to two people.

We all want to know we are loved. A few moments out of our day can make a huge impact on others, and it usually benefits the giver too.

Prayer: *Heavenly Father, thank you for all you do for us. Help us not to grow weary in passing your love and kindness on to others. Amen*

Thought for the day: Who needs an act of kindness from me today?

Doug Brady (Alabama, US)

Happily ever after

Read Psalm 119:105–112

You are good, and what you do is good; teach me your decrees.
Psalm 119:68 (NIV)

I sighed when I read another devotion where a life was at risk, people prayed and the life was miraculously restored. Of course I'm glad for them, but I wondered, 'Where are the voices of those who trust God despite unanswered prayers?'

My husband and I prayed for our children even before they were born. We dedicated them to God, took them to church, taught them scripture and sacrificed so they could have Christian educations. Our family served God with joy. But we still suffered.

Our oldest son drowned as a teenager. After ten years of marriage, our oldest daughter's husband left her. Our youngest son was diagnosed with schizophrenia. It's been three years since our youngest daughter has spoken to us.

Life is hard. Loved ones might die despite our faith and prayer. We may get divorced even when we trust. Diseases can be incurable or fatal. We may pray, live faithfully and trust God, yet still face unthinkable tragedies.

But even knowing this, we can continue to pray and live for God – to believe that God is good, right and lovely, and that God's ways are peace. Even when things go wrong, God is still by our side in the struggle. And we can find joy in knowing we are never alone.

Prayer: *Dear God, thank you for your presence with us. Help us to remain faithful to you, no matter our circumstances. Amen*

Thought for the day: I can always rely on God's presence in my life.

DeVonna R. Allison (Florida, US)

Perseverance

Read Luke 10:38–42

You shall love the Lord your God with all your heart, and with all your soul, and with all your might.

Deuteronomy 6:5 (NRSV)

Sometimes I don't feel like going to worship services. My most frequent excuse is that I did not prepare the right clothes. But then a friend asked me, 'Would you use the same excuse if you didn't feel like going to work?' When it comes to my job, I do everything in my power to find the right clothing and avoid being absent. My friend's question made me pause. So I got ready and went to the worship service.

In Luke 10, Mary took time away from her daily chores to listen to God. It seems to me that we can often be willing to make sacrifices to please ourselves and others. But our love for God should always bring us back to the altar, because he first loved us (see 1 John 4:19).

Worshipping God is an act of perseverance and gratitude for what God does in our lives. As the psalmist says, 'He who keeps Israel will neither slumber nor sleep. The Lord is your keeper; the Lord is your shade at your right hand' (Psalm 121:4–5, NRSV).

Prayer: *Lord Jesus, help us to adore you untiringly and faithfully as we pray the prayer you taught us, 'Our Father which art in heaven, Hallowed be thy name. Thy kingdom come. Thy will be done, as in heaven, so in earth. Give us day by day our daily bread. And forgive us our sins; for we also forgive every one that is indebted to us. And lead us not into temptation; but deliver us from evil.'* Amen*

Thought for the day: Even when it feels inconvenient, I will worship God.

Tomás Adão Calomba (Luanda, Angola)

PRAYER FOCUS: FOR PERSEVERANCE IN MY FAITH

*Luke 11:2–4 (KJV)

Unexpected love

Read Psalm 119:73–80

The human mind may devise many plans, but it is the purpose of the Lord that will be established.

Proverbs 19:21 (NRSV)

When my husband and I celebrated our 40th wedding anniversary, we retraced some of our memories with a trip to New York City, where we were married. We stayed at the same hotel, attended the church where we had met and gotten married, and took a carriage ride through Central Park. But one of the most memorable experiences, totally unplanned and spontaneous, was meeting the 99-year-old pianist who still played the piano regularly at the hotel's restaurant. He came over to our table during our meal and said that he wanted to write us a song for our anniversary. And so he did, and he also played 'Anniversary Waltz'. It has become a new cherished memory that we have added to all our others.

Like that musician, God has a way of surprising us with unplanned and even unimaginable things: the people who came out to greet Jesus as he entered Jerusalem, the disciples who expected the same Passover supper and those who plotted to kill Jesus because he disagreed with them. But God surprised all of them with an unexpected end to the story of Jesus. God gave them and us a new experience, a new outlook and a new and eternal life.

Prayer: *Dear Lord, help us always to be open and ready for your unexpected plans for us. Amen*

Thought for the day: God's love often shows up in unexpected ways.

Xavia Arndt Sheffield (Pennsylvania, US)

 PRAYER FOCUS: TO NOTICE UNEXPECTED BLESSINGS

A great day

Read Mark 1:29–39

Very early in the morning, while it was still dark, Jesus got up, left the house and went off to a solitary place, where he prayed.
Mark 1:35 (NIV)

'I'm overwhelmed,' I confessed to my boss. I had fallen behind on a number of projects at home and at work. Each day seemed to bring a new high-priority issue to my email inbox, my desk at work or my front door, and I had gotten off track. After listening for a few minutes, my boss replied, 'Every morning, I get up early and decide on the *one* thing that I have to do today in order to have a great day.' He realised he was late for another meeting, so he abruptly ended his time with me. I stayed behind pondering his words and wondering which of the many emails, appointments, meetings, tasks from home or verbal requests was my 'one thing' for the day.

In today's scripture, Jesus got up early – before the disciples stirred or the crowds appeared. In those early hours, he spent time with God. As I read this verse, I felt God showing me once more that 'the *one* thing that I have to do today in order to have a great day' is to start my day letting God love me and loving God in return.

Starting my day with God's word and God's love has made all the difference. Instead of being anxious and overwhelmed, I have a great day when I begin it with God.

Prayer: *Father God, when life's demands distract us, help us to remember the importance of spending regular time in your presence. Amen*

Thought for the day: Spending time with God is the most important thing today.

Cassius Rhue (South Carolina, US)

PRAYER FOCUS: SOMEONE STRESSED AT WORK

Everything I do

Read Matthew 5:1–12

Blessed are you when people revile you and persecute you and utter all kinds of evil against you falsely on my account.
Matthew 5:11 (NRSV)

I became a Christian in my senior year of high school, and my Christian youth leader encouraged me to share my faith with the student body. I was scared, but I knew that I should do it, and I wanted to do it. The day came, and in a trembling voice I told the students of Christ's love. I did not think I had much impact; I was just happy it was over.

But then as I walked home a few days later, I saw a student from my school standing on her porch with an older relative. As I passed, she shouted an insult at me, and they both laughed. It took a while before I realised that her words were mocking my testimony of faith. My knees knocked together, and I continued home meekly, filled with despair. I had never been ridiculed like that.

The next day I read Matthew 5:11. I could not believe my eyes when I saw a description of what I had experienced. Immediately, I was filled with joy. All my sadness left, and I thanked God for being faithful and reminding me that God sees everything I do.

Prayer: *Faithful God, help us to share your word, and strengthen us so that we will not fear ridicule. Amen*

Thought for the day: Even when I face ridicule and persecution, God is with me.

Jacqueline London (Diego Martin, Trinidad and Tobago)

 PRAYER FOCUS: THOSE WHO ARE PERSECUTED FOR THEIR FAITH

Graceful greetings

Read Philippians 4:4–9

Grace to you and peace from God our Father and the Lord Jesus Christ.

Ephesians 1:2 (NRSV)

Unfortunately, the week before Easter I had a disagreement with a parishioner, whom I'll call Steve. When he showed up to worship the next week, I found myself standing in the pulpit at the beginning of worship with my mind flooded with worry about him and about our church, rather than focused on the good news of the resurrection. What a terrible way to start worship on Easter!

On that day I truly understood why in the first few verses of all his letters, Paul starts with something along the lines of today's quoted scripture. He doesn't start with condemnation or correction. He doesn't get to the point of the letter until he has first reached out to them in Christian love, no matter what the situation. So that Easter, during the 'passing of the peace', I made it a point to walk straight from the pulpit towards Steve, shake his hand and say, 'Steve, grace and peace to you in the name of Jesus Christ.' Since that day, I've come to the conclusion that Paul had it right. We will have disagreements with one another, but we can't properly worship God and have true Christian relationships unless we first reach out in love.

When we intentionally make peace, grace and love the priorities in our relationships, our lives begin to look more and more like the life of Jesus.

Prayer: *Loving God, help us to show your love to everyone before we do anything else. Amen*

Thought for the day: When I disagree with someone, I will first reach out in Christian love.

Brennan Hurley (North Carolina, US)

PRAYER FOCUS: SOMEONE I DISAGREE WITH

Finding God in loss

Read John 14:25–27

Do not let your hearts be troubled and do not be afraid.
John 14:27 (NIV)

Jesus comforted his disciples after their last supper together, telling them how he must leave for a while and assuring them they would not be alone. After my husband's suicide, I saw more clearly how the disciples must have felt when faced with the reality of their loss. I could imagine how they waited through interminable moments of the night, hearts quaking with uncertainty and fear as they tried to understand what was to come.

As I drove to and from my assignments for the local newspaper, mourning the loss of my husband, I did not see how I could survive. Drying my eyes to do interviews and take pictures, I recorded the lives of others even as my own seemed to be ending. I questioned and cried out to God, who had been there for everything else in my life. In time, I felt God helping me rebuild my life by sending me other people who had experienced traumatic loss.

Now I can write about the long journey towards healing I have experienced and the blessings I continue to receive. A sense of peace, my grandsons, the support of family and churches, and a connection with others who have lost loved ones to suicide are some of the gifts that have turned my life's greatest tragedy into something powerful and good.

Prayer: *Redeeming God, thank you for turning our mourning into joy. Your love is our most precious gift. In the name of Jesus. Amen*

Thought for the day: When I am broken, God will help me rebuild.

Jan McDaniel (Georgia, US)

 PRAYER FOCUS: FAMILIES AFFECTED BY SUICIDE

Promise of spring

Read Luke 23:39–43

Jesus said unto him, Verily I say unto thee, Today shalt thou be with me in paradise.

Luke 23:43 (KJV)

When I was hiking in the woods one early spring day, the sky was overcast. The scenery was full of bleak, leafless trees. As I climbed a hill, a gust of wind turned my thoughts to sadness and melancholy. God seemed far away from me at that moment.

But suddenly I saw an unexpected sight: a tiny blue wildflower peeking up at me from a pile of dead leaves. At once my melancholy and loneliness left my heart. Spring was already on its way, and God was sending me a message even as I had felt far from God.

Even when God's blessings seem distant, the promises of God – like the promise of spring – will be fulfilled. When we remember these promises while waiting on God, they can become more evident. We can give thanks to God and remember Jesus' promise to the man next to him as they were both dying at Golgotha: Paradise is coming!

Prayer: *Dear Lord, help us keep our eyes on your brightness and glory when the world seems dark. In Jesus' name. Amen*

Thought for the day: Even in times of sadness, God sends messages of hope and joy.

Gary E. Crum (Virginia, US)

In its time

Read Ecclesiastes 3:1–14

[God] has made everything beautiful in its time.

Ecclesiastes 3:11 (NIV)

For years, I struggled to reconcile my ambitions and notions of success with God's timing and plan for my life. As a musician and songwriter, comparing myself to others in my field and what they were achieving was a perpetual snare.

Then during an extended maternity leave following the birth of my second son, I wrestled with the financial and physical constraints of raising two small children in a single-income home. Laying aside my career ambitions in order to care for my kids was painful. I was living my long-awaited dream of being at home with my children full time, but I struggled with a real sense of loss. I feared I was letting my life waste away while accomplishing nothing. It took a long time for me to begin seeing things differently.

The writer of Ecclesiastes described something profound about the nature of God's timing. God fulfils each beautiful promise to God's children in its time. Some flowers bloom earlier and others bloom later, but they all have their moment of beauty and glory. In the same way, God's timing is never a punishment but a distinguishing mark of our unique purpose.

Prayer: *Heavenly Father, help us to see your timing as a gift rather than a punishment. Strengthen us so that we can participate with you in your timing. Amen*

Thought for the day: I will measure my success according to God's word.

Katie Overbeek (Ontario, Canada)

He lives

Read 1 Peter 1:3–9

Since death came through a man, the resurrection of the dead comes also through a man. For as in Adam all die, so in Christ all will be made alive.

1 Corinthians 15:21–22 (NIV)

My wife showed me an obituary that a friend had sent to her. It was shockingly brief; it simply gave the man's name, where he lived and then said, 'He died.' Two words summed up a life of 65 years.

My initial reaction was that an obituary so short showed a lack of compassion. But perhaps there were other factors involved – no money to pay for a longer summary or no close family survivors with details. And then I thought about Jesus' death over 2,000 years ago. Jesus Christ was arrested and tried as a criminal. He was found guilty, tortured and then suffered humiliating crucifixion. Perhaps in the days following Good Friday, if someone asked what happened to Jesus, the response may have simply been, 'He died.'

Until Jesus, death was the last chapter of life, the end of the story. But Jesus changed everything when he rose from the dead on Easter Sunday. As Paul writes in Romans, 'Through Christ Jesus the law of the Spirit who gives life has set you free from the law of sin and death' (Romans 8:2, NIV). In the case of Christ, the summary is, 'He lives.' Because he lives, he offers eternal life to all who believe and follow him.

Prayer: *Dear Father, thank you for the gift of your Son, Jesus Christ. Help us to prepare for eternal life by serving others and bringing glory to your name. Amen*

Thought for the day: For all who believe in Christ, death is not the last word.

John D. Bown (Minnesota, US)

Time well spent

Read 1 Kings 19:9–12

After the earthquake a fire; but the Lord was not in the fire: and after the fire a still small voice.

1 Kings 19:12 (KJV)

While brushing my teeth one morning, instead of pondering what I needed to accomplish that day I began mentally reciting a scripture I had memorised. God used that moment to show me something in a Bible verse that I had never noticed, enhancing my understanding and filling me with gratitude.

I marvel that God would teach me during such a mundane task. How wondrously God created our minds, to be able to perform routine chores without thinking about them so that we can focus our thoughts on other matters! I usually fill everyday activities with my own plans for the day, instead of quietly seeking God's wisdom and direction. How often do I miss God's still small voice because of my planning?

I no longer dread daily tasks I once thought boring or unimportant. Instead, I have come to see them as opportunities to quiet my thoughts and focus on God in prayer and meditation. God can use those times to draw me closer, teaching me, inspiring me and strengthening my life of discipleship.

Prayer: *Dear God, forgive us when we crowd you out of our daily routines. Help us to use even the mundane tasks of each day to focus on you and your wisdom. Amen*

Thought for the day: Everyday tasks can be time spent in God's presence.

Judy Ransom (Florida, US)

God restores

Read Psalm 51:13–17

The sacrifices of God are a broken spirit: a broken and a contrite heart, O God, thou wilt not despise.

Psalm 51:17 (KJV)

Today's reading is from a psalm of David, the king of Israel. It reflects his thoughts after he has realised the gravity and implications of conspiracy against Uriah the Hittite and his adultery with Bathsheba, Uriah's wife. His actions result in a baby boy, and God rebukes David through the prophet Nathan (see 2 Samuel 11–12).

In the psalm, David's broken heart is obvious. He has realised that he has sinned against God, whom he loves. He fears being separated from God because of his actions. Despite the consequences he suffered, God restored David's life.

In 2007, when I was 21 years old, my heart felt burdened with sin. I decided to go to church the next Sunday to seek redemption. I was broken inside and felt hopeless. But every word the pastor preached spoke directly to my heart. That moment marked my life forever. The joy and the love for God I felt were indescribable. David's story reassures me that no matter how broken we are, God can restore us all.

Prayer: *Father in heaven, thank you for your mercy and the way you restore our lives. Amen.*

Thought for the day: God's love can restore anyone.

Albert Dob (Bucharest, Romania)

Commitment

Read Matthew 22:34–39

Surely I am with you always.

Matthew 28:20 (NIV)

Years ago, a church-planting friend advised me that the key to growing a successful church is to remain focused on Jesus' command to love God and one another and his instruction to make disciples. As we prepared to launch our new church, we wanted to stay focused on these principles. The journey has been anything but easy, but Jesus reminds us daily, 'I am with you always.'

At our church, we try to think about reaching one person, one family, at a time. So every day our church is intentional about meeting new people – sharing our story and, more importantly, listening to theirs. We go regularly to schools, cinemas, restaurants, bars, parks and community outings – listening. And as we listen, loving connections are formed.

Our commitment to loving God and neighbour and to making disciples has helped us to grow a strong church.

Prayer: *Dear God, give us the strength daily to share your story of love with another person. In Jesus' name. Amen*

Thought for the day: In what small way can I show love to a neighbour today?

Teddy Rollins (Georgia, US)

Gather your elephants

Read 1 Peter 5:1–11

Be alert and of sober mind. Your enemy the devil prowls around like a roaring lion looking for someone to devour.

1 Peter 5:8 (NIV)

Newborn African elephants are susceptible to attacks from predators like lions and hyenas. As a mother elephant gives birth, the herd gathers to protect her and the newborn.

My daughter's family is going through a difficult time. For us, gathered elephants symbolise the protection of her community and prayer. A small wooden elephant sits by my kitchen sink. My daughter's friend gave her two small elephant figurines when she moved away, knowing that the days ahead could leave my daughter vulnerable. The elephants serve as a reminder that she is not alone. When she feels overwhelmed by her situation, the elephants remind her of the community that will support her with prayer whatever comes her way.

When a hard day hits, my daughter gathers her community by texting me, her sisters and her friends who immediately surround her with prayer.

Scripture tells us to be alert, because evil prowls like a roaring lion. But God has not left us defenceless in our times of vulnerability and pain. In those times, we can ask others to gather around us and pray for us.

Prayer: *Dear Lord, help us to share our struggles with those who surround and encourage us through prayer. Amen*

Thought for the day: Today I will support a friend through prayer.

Glenda Moore (Illinois, US)

PRAYER FOCUS: FRIENDS WHO PRAY FOR ONE ANOTHER

Spiritual food

Read Psalm 1:1–3

Do not… take your Holy Spirit from me.

Psalm 51:11 (NIV)

I've always considered reading to be spiritual food and a daily treat. Early in my life it became not only a treat but a tool to build up my inner strength. I nurtured my soul by starting my day reading the wisdom of great artists and thinkers. It was a way to steel myself for my everyday challenges. I'd leave for school with deep calmness, but then as the day progressed and challenges arose, it was difficult to implement the lessons of my daily reading.

At the time I didn't realise that I could not find answers to 'how' questions – like how to live, how to endure and how to act – with wisdom, philosophy, tradition, art and science alone. I needed the comfort that faith brings.

When I got to know the living God as a young adult, I finally understood. Before, I had regarded the Bible as an excellent collection of writings. But through faith in God, it opened up before me. I have made daily Bible reading a practice for about 30 years now with joy every morning. The word of God, which helps us find real answers to the 'how' questions and gives real strength, is our daily spiritual food.

Prayer: *Holy Spirit, come into our hearts and nurture us with wisdom and strength. Amen*

Thought for the day: I can find wisdom and strength in God's word.

Zoltán Szügyi (Budapest, Hungary)

Sunflowers

Read Matthew 8:18–22

I am the light of the world. Whoever follows me will never walk in darkness, but will have the light of life.
John 8:12 (NIV)

When I take a morning run in the summer, I pass a field with row after row of sunflowers. It is a breathtaking sight. One overcast morning, I noticed that every sunflower was facing downward towards the ground. This led me to do some research, and I learned that sunflowers likely earned their name for two reasons. First, their physical appearance resembles the sun. And second, the faces of young sunflowers follow the sun as it moves throughout the day, something called heliotropism. The sun wasn't shining that day, so the sunflowers were not keeping their heads up.

How many times in our spiritual lives are we like the sunflowers? It is easy to look to God when we see God's wonders around us. But when life gets messy, it can be difficult to see God working. We may hang our heads and let our hearts turn away from God. Trusting in God and waiting patiently for God's answer can be the hardest things that we face on our spiritual journey. However, we can keep our eyes fixed on God and follow where God leads, even on cloudy days.

Prayer: *Dear Lord, thank you for the light and guidance that you provide for us. Help us to keep our eyes and hearts fixed on you. Amen*

Thought for the day: How am I following God's light today?

Julie Sipe (Pennsylvania, US)

Without envy

Read 1 Samuel 18:6–16

Love is patient, love is kind. It does not envy, it does not boast, it is not proud.

1 Corinthians 13:4 (NIV)

My friend Emily suffers from cystic fibrosis, a degenerative lung disease. She often wheezes and has laboured breathing, and she periodically sees a specialist to determine if she is a candidate for a lung transplant.

One day I told Emily about a cystic fibrosis patient who had markers that qualified him for a new, promising medication. Unfortunately, Emily does not have the same markers, so the treatment wouldn't be effective for her. But she was overjoyed for him. She didn't ask, 'Why not me?' or display any envy. I'm not sure I would be so gracious in her position.

When the people started to love David more than Saul, King Saul was consumed with envy and tried to murder him. In contrast, John the Baptist knew his ministry and followers would diminish when Jesus appeared, yet he delighted in the Messiah's coming.

I want to be like John rather than like Saul. When I feel envious, I can remember that God's love, power and forgiveness abound. Someone else being blessed does not diminish God's ability or willingness to bless me. God's goodness and mercy are unlimited and always available.

Prayer: *Merciful God, forgive us when we envy. Reveal to us any envy in our hearts, and change our thoughts and hearts to love more like you. Amen*

Thought for the day: God can transform my heart and replace envy with love.

Lin Daniels (Massachusetts, US)

Family time

Read Mark 3:31–35

Looking at those who sat around him, [Jesus] said, 'Here are my mother and my brothers! Whoever does the will of God is my brother and sister and mother.'
Mark 3:34–35 (NRSV)

In Mark 3, Jesus' family members were looking for him when he was among the people, teaching them the word of God. When Jesus heard that his family members were searching for him, he responded by saying that his mother and brothers were seated around him and listening to him. Jesus did not allow his family members to draw him away from his spiritual family because he saw the necessity of giving his time to both his families. He had dedicated this time to his spiritual family.

I love the time I spend around my own family, but I also realise the need to spend time with my church family. When I have the opportunity to spend time with my spiritual family, I do not allow others to distract me. And however busy I may be, I make time for my spiritual family. Through fellowship with them, I receive encouragement and nourishment as we share the word of God. Through Jesus Christ, we are members of God's family and in that family we experience joy.

Prayer: *Dear Lord, remind us of our need to spend time with our spiritual family. Help us to make spiritual fellowship a priority. In Jesus' name. Amen*

Thought for the day: Spending time with my spiritual family renews my faith.

Enid Adah Nyinomujuni (Dar es Salaam, Tanzania)

Enthusiastic response

Read Romans 12:9–13

Never be lacking in zeal, but keep your spiritual fervour, serving the Lord.

Romans 12:11 (NIV)

A young family walked to the chancel for an infant baptism as our congregation waited expectantly. Two parents, their infant son and their four-year-old daughter, Sydney, gathered around the baptismal font. I asked the parents numerous questions of commitment during the baptismal vows. Each time they replied, 'We do.' After every response, Sydney exclaimed, 'Me too!'

The congregation was surprised and delighted by her eagerness. Sydney's obvious enthusiasm and desire to be a part of this significant occasion caused me to reflect later: How do I demonstrate my zeal for following Christ? How do I convey the joy and excitement that a relationship with God brings me?

In today's reading, Paul encourages the Romans to maintain their spiritual fervour and to serve the Lord. God invites us to experience the adventure of living for Christ every day. May we respond with gratitude, dedication and zeal.

Prayer: *Dear God, thank you those who enthusiastically show their devotion to you. We pray as Jesus taught us, 'Our Father in heaven, hallowed be your name, your kingdom come, your will be done, on earth as it is in heaven. Give us today our daily bread. And forgive us our debts, as we also have forgiven our debtors. And lead us not into temptation, but deliver us from the evil one.' Amen*

Thought for the day: When my zeal is lacking, God can use others to encourage me.

Jim Bell (North Carolina, US)

 PRAYER FOCUS: OLDER SIBLINGS

*Matthew 6:9–13

Love and protection

Read Psalm 4:4–8

This is the day that the Lord has made; let us rejoice and be glad in it.
Psalm 118:24 (NRSV)

In 2016, my husband and I took our two teenage granddaughters on a trip to Alaska. As we settled into our seats for the first leg of our flight there, I handed out small notebooks to use as personal journals during the trip. On the first page of each notebook, I had written two Bible verses: today's quoted verse from Psalm 118 and a verse from today's reading: 'In peace I will lie down and sleep, for you alone, Lord, make me dwell in safety' (Psalm 4:8, NIV).

Each morning we recited Psalm 118:24. It set the tone for our days filled with opportunities to enjoy the scenery and creatures of Alaska. Each evening as we settled down to sleep, we would recite Psalm 4:8. It was a calming practice as we relaxed in the knowledge that God was with us and would protect us as we slept.

Since that memorable trip, I have continued to repeat these Bible verses each morning and night. I find that reciting Psalm 4:8 focuses my mind on God's presence and peace. Despite the worries of the day, God is with me. The cares of the world slip away, and my sleep comes more quickly. These two verses have become the bookends for my days, and my life is all the sweeter for this daily practice.

Prayer: *Heavenly Father, thank you for the opportunity to rejoice and be glad for the wonderful world you have given us and for the peace of knowing your love and protection are with us even as we sleep. Amen*

Thought for the day: When I wake and when I sleep, I will be mindful of God's blessings.

Carol Shaw Johnston (Tennessee, US)

PRAYER FOCUS: THOSE WHO SUFFER FROM INSOMNIA

God's faithfulness

Read Matthew 9:18–26

Jesus replied, 'Didn't I tell you that if you believe, you will see God's glory?'

John 11:40 (CEB)

I remember the indescribable emotion I felt the first time I heard the heartbeat of my soon-to-be-born daughter. The next day, I accompanied my wife to the doctor's office for a checkup. The exhilaration of the day before suddenly turned into fear: The doctor said that our daughter's life was at risk. I was stunned, my faith shaken. Many fearful thoughts crossed my mind.

But that moment passed quickly when I remembered that God had always sustained me in my life's journey. I knew that if I remained rooted in my belief that God is constantly with me, I could face whatever came. In today's reading, the synagogue leader's faith was strong in spite of the death of his daughter. His faith led him to believe in the power of Jesus to restore her to life.

We will face doubts and difficult situations. But God wants only the best for us – full lives following the path Jesus Christ has set. We can be certain that in all circumstances God will sustain us and remain faithfully by our side.

Prayer: *O God, thank you for your steadfast faithfulness in good times and in times of adversity. Amen*

Thought for the day: God's faithfulness to me is unwavering.

Jairón Otoniel Santana Suárez (Dominican Republic)

Noble work

Read Genesis 4:7–22

Whatever you do, you should do it all for God's glory.

1 Corinthians 10:31 (CEB)

Recently some local high school students were returning home from a maths competition when the brakes went out on their bus. The driver took her foot off the accelerator and slowly made her way to the shoulder of the road, eventually stopping just a few feet from a ditch. Then she called for help and kept an eye on the students until help arrived. This experienced driver was praised for staying calm in a dangerous situation and for acting on her training.

I thought about how bus drivers don't usually receive accolades for their work, even though they have an extremely important job. Many of our daily tasks seem mundane, and it's only during events like these that we learn to appreciate the people who carry them out.

Genesis 4:19–22 speaks of the descendants of Cain and the talents God gave them. Among these gifts were raising livestock, playing instruments and working with metal. These gifts don't seem like holy callings in themselves, but any task done for the Lord becomes a noble one. Paul teaches us, 'Whatever you do, you should do it all for God's glory.' When we heed these words, we invite God to use us to draw others to our creator, even when our efforts seem mundane.

Prayer: *Dear Lord, help us always to remember to use our talents for your glory. In Jesus' name. Amen*

Thought for the day: Whatever my work, I can do it for God.

Jody Williams (Illinois, US)

Grace and comfort

Read Matthew 6:25–34

Do not worry about your life, what you will eat or drink; or about your body, what you will wear. Is not life more than food, and the body more than clothes?

Matthew 6:25 (NIV)

I remember the day in 2008 when my dad lost his company to bankruptcy. All I could hear was the frustration in my dad's voice, but eight-year-old me didn't really understand what was happening. I always wanted to be just like my dad, but I found myself lost and confused.

As days passed my dad searched for a new job. Each day I would ask with hope in my voice, 'Did you get the job?' But every time, the answer was no. As his search continued, I started to lose hope; I wondered why God was putting my family through these hardships. Through the weeks my dad started to notice the change in my tone of voice when he would come back from an interview. When he noticed my hope fading, he told me, 'Brayan, I know what we are going through is different and hard, but you need to know that God will always provide for us – somehow, some way.'

I learned that even when we struggle, God gives love, relief and opportunities throughout life. I have had much and I have had little, but the amount of grace and comfort that God has provided for me has never changed.

Prayer: *Dear God, thank you for all that you provide for us. Help us to recognise your blessings in tough times. Amen*

Thought for the day: Today I will look for God's blessings in my life.

Brayan Orellana (Texas, US)

Let it happen

Read Acts 16:6–15

May the God of peace himself cause you to be completely dedicated to him… The one who is calling you is faithful and will do this.

1 Thessalonians 5:23–24 (CEB)

I was excited to attend a conference in California. While praying about the trip, I sensed God preparing me to share the gospel with a passenger on my flight.

My seatmate was a woman named Nadia, who had been on a nine-month solo world tour. California was her last stop before she returned home to Australia. As we chatted over lunch, our conversation flowed naturally from one subject to another, and somehow the topic of faith arose. I didn't push; she didn't resist. It simply happened.

I talked about Jesus and how important he is to me. And like a rose unfolding its petals, Nadia opened her heart to him. We joined hands and prayed.

At the luggage carousel, the friends that I was travelling with welcomed Nadia into God's family. Nadia and I hugged, and I encouraged her to read the Bible and find a church back home.

It's in my nature to fuss over how events might unfold. But that day I learned that I don't have to push doors open; I can let God open them gently.

Prayer: *Dear Lord, when we worry about how we can share the good news with others, help us trust you to prepare the way. Amen*

Thought for the day: Today, I will share my faith when God opens the door.

Rose McCormick Brandon (Ontario, Canada)

PRAYER FOCUS: FOR OPPORTUNITIES TO SHARE THE GOSPEL

U-turns allowed

Read Deuteronomy 31:1–8

Show me your ways, Lord, teach me your paths.
Psalm 25:4 (NIV)

At the sound of screeching tyres, we checked the rear-view mirror and saw our 90-year-old uncle making a U-turn on a crowded street. He continued to tail our car despite the congested traffic, and he used hand gestures to tell us where to go. Ten minutes earlier, my sister Marianne and I had waved goodbye after a visit with him and our aunt. Our uncle had given us directions around the construction, but the city was unfamiliar to us and we had forgotten his instructions. We were shocked to find he was following us to ensure we made it safely past the roadblocks!

His actions reminded me of the way God never abandons us. God stays with us and guides us on right paths. We may encounter roadblocks, like marital difficulties, money problems or addictions, but God provides guidance to help us navigate even the bumpiest of circumstances.

Praying, applying scripture to our situations and praising God before we see results are like making a U-turn. They make space for God to move our lives in the direction God desires for us.

Prayer: *Precious Lord, thank you for giving us new opportunities and fresh starts. Help us to follow your paths instead of our own. Amen*

Thought for the day: Following God's guidance can turn my life around.

Jeanie Jacobson (Nebraska, US)

Our all

Read Colossians 3:23–25

Whatever you do, work at it with all your heart, as working for the Lord, not for human masters.

Colossians 3:23 (NIV)

When I entered high school, it seemed like everyone already knew one another. I felt alone and insecure. At lunch and in classes, I watched and studied the way other students talked and how they treated one another. Hearing talk of sex, drugs and violence disappointed me and made me worry.

Each day I prayed for my high school and asked God to use me. After a week of praying, God prompted me to start a prayer circle. I was nervous and scared I would be judged, but I trusted God. I began to pray every morning in the front lobby. Some days people would pray with me, and other days I would stand by myself. As I continued to pray, I felt God speaking to me again. I was only following God's guidance within my comfort zone; I wasn't giving my all to what God had called me to do. So I put up flyers throughout the school and posted the information about the prayer circle on social media. I asked other students to help spread the word. By the end of that year, more than 30 of us prayed together almost every day.

When God calls us, we often do the bare minimum and then blame God when things don't work out. But God asks us to give all of ourselves to our work. No matter what we do for God, we can give it our all – just as God does for us.

Prayer: *Dear God, give us the strength and motivation we need to work for your kingdom. Amen*

Thought for the day: In whatever work God calls me to do, I will give my all.

Joey Ortiz (Texas, US)

Pray continually

Read Romans 8:26–28

Give thanks in all circumstances; for this is the will of God in Christ Jesus for you.

1 Thessalonians 5:18 (NRSV)

I was going through a difficult situation. The thought of recent events made me so scared that I could barely sleep. Every morning I woke up feeling weak and fearful just thinking of my problem. For a while I pretended that everything was all right, but that hurt me even more. I was desperate for a shoulder to lean on so I could cry out my fears and seek guidance. That's when I realised that I could pray to God.

So each day I knelt down to pray. Each time I would immediately start crying because the situation was too overwhelming for me to speak of. I did this for many days, and I started to feel better. Eventually I was able to tell God what had happened and how I felt. Though my pain didn't completely go away, I realised that the fear didn't rule over me anymore.

Today I realise that every problem I have encountered has made me trust and rely on God more. By praying continually, I found relief from my fears. No matter how bad life gets, we can always pray to God, 'the author and finisher of our faith' (Hebrews 12:2, KJV).

Prayer: *Dear God, help us remember to pray and to trust you no matter how bad life gets for us. Amen*

Thought for the day: Even when my prayers have no words, God is listening.

Keren Philips (Karnataka, India)

The labyrinth

Read Psalm 16:5–11

Trust in the Lord with all your heart and lean not on your own understanding.
Proverbs 3:5 (NIV)

I've always loved to walk a prayer labyrinth. The calming repetitiveness of the various switchbacks and turns of the path lulls me into a meditative state. Over the years my affection for the prayer walk or labyrinth has remained. When you walk a labyrinth it is not always clear how or when you will reach the centre, but you trust the path will lead you there. If you step out of the path or don't follow the turns, however, you may not reach the centre at all. You have to be mindful of following the track and trusting it to lead you to the end.

Proverbs 3:5 tells us to trust and rely on the Lord rather than on ourselves. Life is much like a labyrinth in this way. God counts on us to follow the path without cutting corners and making careless mistakes. Sometimes we do not know where God is leading us or how we will get there, but we can trust that God will lead us along the path.

Prayer: *Dear God, thank you for leading us on the path of life. Help us to remain on it faithfully. Amen*

Thought for the day: God provides us a path to follow and trusts us to follow it.

Abigail Mills (Arizona, US)

Renewed life

Read Colossians 3:12–17

Do not be conformed to this world, but be transformed by the renewing of your minds, so that you may discern what is the will of God – what is good and acceptable and perfect.

Romans 12:2 (NRSV)

When I learned about the metamorphosis of butterflies, I was amazed. I find caterpillars to be unpleasant – especially those that sting when you touch them. But it is through the caterpillar that we get the gentle and beautiful butterfly. The transformation is a miracle. And once the metamorphosis has happened, we don't remember the caterpillar; we simply enjoy the beauty of the butterfly.

It's the same in my life. I think I have 'caterpillars' in me that sting others and make them dislike being close to me. It is difficult to get rid of negative feelings and behaviours, but as a follower of Christ, I must be willing to change. With the help of the Holy Spirit, I can cast off feelings of inferiority, anger and selfishness. It takes time, and the process is not easy, but in doing so I can follow Paul's advice: 'Do not be conformed to this world, but be transformed by the renewing of your minds.'

Prayer: *Dear God, help us to let go of negative feelings and behaviours. By your power transform our lives into things of beauty. Amen*

Thought for the day: When I am willing to change, God can transform my life.

Merry Gultom (West Java, Indonesia)

Abundant blessings

Read Philippians 4:10–20

God is able to bless you abundantly, so that in all things at all times, having all that you need, you will abound in every good work.
2 Corinthians 9:8 (NIV)

I keep a memo on my phone where I note the date and situation whenever I sense God's presence and guidance. I began this practice a little over two years ago, and I now have thousands of entries. Sometimes, in the busyness of life, we neglect to see God's work in the minutiae. Even if we feel God's presence in the large events, recognising that God leads us and helps us in the smallest ways can sometimes mean the most.

Scrolling back through my list, I remember that God has been there for me every second of every day, and I should live accordingly in my actions and words. No action is too small for us to feel God's influence. If we take the time to acknowledge it, we will recognise God's involvement in every aspect of our lives.

Prayer: *Heavenly Father, help us not to lose sight of the blessings you have given us. Remind us that the greatest gifts can come in the smallest ways. Help us to focus on your influence in our lives. Amen*

Thought for the day: Today I will notice God's work in the smallest blessings of my life.

Andrew Sulgit (West Virginia, US)

Seeing clearly

Read 1 Corinthians 13:1–13

For now we see through a glass, darkly; but then face to face: now I know in part; but then shall I know even as also I am known.
1 Corinthians 13:12 (KJV)

For several years I was aware that my eyesight was deteriorating. Cataracts were the diagnosis. However, an operation was not an option until the problem had developed sufficiently to make such action practicable. I could see well enough to go about my daily business, or so I thought.

Eventually the day came and the operation was carried out. I was amazed by the results. For the first time in years, I could see clearly and once again marvel at God's creation.

Spiritual life can be a bit like that. We may think that we can see clearly. I attended Sunday school, Bible class and Boys Brigade, and later attended church occasionally but took no active part in its activities. One day, however, I was out walking in the countryside with two friends who were both involved in church youth work. When they asked me if I would like to join them and become a Sunday school teacher, I declined emphatically and lagged behind. At that point, however, I suddenly realised that all I had learned about the Lord as a child was, in fact, actually true. It was as though a mist had cleared from my eyes and I could see clearly.

I caught up with my friends and told them I would be joining them on Sunday morning. I have served the Lord ever since.

Prayer: *Dear Lord, we know that when we look to Jesus, he will carry us through.*

Thought for the day: We only see through a glass, darkly, until we see Jesus and give our lives to him.

William Findlay (Scotland, United Kingdom)

 PRAYER FOCUS: OPHTHALMIC SURGEONS

Call on God

Read Psalm 126

Jesus began to weep.

John 11:35 (NRSV)

When we said goodbye to my sister at the airport, we had no idea the difficulties she would face. She was young and had chosen a medical course at a boarding school. And it is never easy to live far from family and friends.

She often called our mother to cry, saying that she wanted to quit the course. But our mother and I gave her what strength and encouragement we could. I had also attended boarding school, so I knew how difficult it can be to cry and not have a shoulder to lean on.

After more than eight years, I was glad to see my sister dressed in her graduation gown and our mother dancing and singing songs of jubilation. I thought back to the many times our mother wept from seeing her daughter almost undernourished because of her study schedule.

Sometimes as we go through difficulties we feel that our whole life will be hard. But just as my sister called us to cry over her fears, I have learned that we can also call on God. Through prayer we can share our struggles with God and find relief from any situation. Regardless of the difficulties we face, God always holds our hand.

Prayer: *Dear God, thank you for listening to our prayers in times of difficulty. In your Son's name we pray. Amen*

Thought for the day: Prayer can lighten my burdens and bring me peace.

Hélder Moisés Mangumo (Maputo, Mozambique)

Choosing God

Read Isaiah 48:17–19

If only you had paid attention to my commands, your peace would have been like a river, your well-being like the waves of the sea.
Isaiah 48:18 (NIV)

My family and I live close to the Gulf of Mexico. I love to walk along the beautiful beaches of white sands and emerald green water. When I see and hear the waves of the ocean crashing on the sand, I feel incredible peace and joy at being so close to nature and to God. I often say to my husband, 'We should come here every day.' But despite the beach's proximity, we rarely go. The responsibilities of work, home and family take up most of our time. We forgo the natural beauty of the shoreline to walk around our neighbourhood, often following the same path each day. While our neighbourhood is lovely, it does not compare to the seashore or to the peace that I find there.

My spiritual life is similar. Like the ocean, God is always nearby. God is only a prayer away, regardless of my location, yet I often forget to read the Bible or visit with God. When I don't make spending time with God a priority, I miss out on the peace and wisdom that comes from daily Bible study.

Fortunately, each day brings a new opportunity to choose the peace and well-being God offers through praying and reading the Bible. The gift of God's power and peace comes when we choose to devote ourselves to time with God ahead of everything else.

Prayer: *Dear God, teach us what is best for us, and direct us in the way we should go. Amen*

Thought for the day: I can renew my mind when I spend time with God each day.

Cathy Lee Taylor (Florida, US)

Representing Christ

Read 2 Timothy 2:3–5, 22–23

We are ambassadors for Christ, since God is making his appeal through us.

2 Corinthians 5:20 (NRSV)

We were halfway through army basic training. Before being dismissed for our first 24-hour town leave, our drill instructor reminded us: 'Remember, each of you represents the US army to whomever you meet and in whatever you do. If you are caught in a compromising position that reflects poorly on our army, we will hear about it. You have to answer to me.' As demanding as our drill instructor was, we knew he had our best interest at heart. We didn't want to disappoint him or tarnish the army's image of disciplined soldiers.

In a similar way, we represent Jesus after we accept him as our Lord and Saviour. Whenever we interact with anyone – at a store, where we work, when eating out or when we answer the phone – we represent Christ. Do we treat store clerks and service workers with respect and try to make them feel appreciated and valued? Do we represent Christ well every day and in every way? After all, Jesus loves everyone because we are all God's children.

Prayer: *Dear Lord, help us remember that we represent you wherever we are and to everyone we meet. Amen*

Thought for the day: How will I represent Christ today?

Leland P. Gamson (Arizona, US)

New understanding

Read John 3:14–21

Whoever believes in him is not condemned, but whoever does not believe stands condemned already because they have not believed in the name of God's one and only Son.

John 3:18 (NIV)

I grew up without going to church or learning about God. As an adult, when I was expecting my third child, I found my dad's Bible among his things after his death. I looked at the verses he had underlined, hoping to know him better. One of those was John 3:16. I read today's quoted verse too and learned that if I did not believe in the name of Jesus Christ I was under judgement. But then I wondered, 'Why should I believe?' When I once asked God for something, I got no answer.

The word 'judgement' was often in my thoughts after that. I could not remember all that I had read from the verses, but that word stood out. I started to dwell on it. I began to worry about terrible things happening to me as a result of God's judgement, like dying in childbirth or losing my son. I dreamed about it at night. For months, these thoughts brought me misery.

But then my child was born healthy. When I came home from the hospital, I read John 3 again and came upon verse 16: 'For God so loved the world…' It was as if I had missed those words before! For several months, I had been afraid of something I had misunderstood. Now when I read the Bible and do not understand something, I bring it before God in prayer.

Prayer: *Loving God, as I read the Bible, help me to understand your word. Amen*

Thought for the day: Today I will seek new understanding from familiar scriptures.

Pál Tünde (Pest, Hungary)

Why are we surprised?

Read Mark 11:22–25

Therefore I tell you, whatever you ask for in prayer, believe that you have received it, and it will be yours.

Mark 11:24 (NIV)

On a family vacation to the Black Hills of South Dakota, we were on a winding road that was popular with tourists because of the wild donkeys that often graze on the forested hillsides. We had talked about seeing the donkeys for days, and our five-year-old son was anxiously anticipating this experience. After driving for over an hour around the donkey area marked on a tourist map, I told our son that we would have to give up on our search. From the back seat I heard this quiet prayer: 'Please, God, help my daddy find the donkeys.'

My heart sank. How could I tell a five-year-old that God does not always answer prayer the way that we expect? As I was beginning a shaky explanation, we rounded a curve and saw a dozen donkeys dotting the hillside. The white-muzzled creatures began nibbling the dried grass on the shoulder of the road. Squeals of delight erupted from the back seat. Just as I was limiting God's power, our son's prayer was answered. Did I even stop to think that God might respond to our son's prayer? Certainly I was not expecting to see the donkeys. In today's verse, Jesus assures us, 'Whatever you ask for in prayer, believe that you have received it, and it will be yours.' Why are we surprised when our prayers are answered?

Prayer: *Loving God, when we pray for guidance and help, fill us with trust as we seek answers. Amen*

Thought for the day: Faith is the cornerstone of my prayers.

David Knisely (Michigan, US)

Small group questions

Wednesday 6 January

1 Do you believe God has one clear path for our lives, and that we can miss the path and be out of God's perfect will? Why or why not? What scripture verses support your answer?

2 In what ways has God blessed your acts of service? How are you encouraged by those blessings?

3 How do you make sure you are seeking God in everything? How can you tell when you are seeking God and when you are not? What spiritual practices keep you focused on God?

4 What gifts and talents can you use to serve others for God? In what ways are you already using those gifts for God? In what new ways would you like to start using your gifts?

5 When have you felt unsure of how to serve God? Who or what helped you find direction? How might you help someone else who is feeling unsure of how to serve?

Wednesday 13 January

1 Describe a time in your life when you have experienced loneliness and rejection. What did you do to combat those feelings?

2 Which verses from today's reading do you most relate to? Why? What verses from other psalms do you find encouraging?

3 Today's writer talks about the loneliness David must have felt in 1 Samuel. What other biblical characters experienced loneliness? What can you learn from their stories?

4 In Psalm 34, David says that God answered him and delivered him from his fears. How might David's experience help you when you are going through a difficult time?

5 When you feel alone and rejected, how does your faith help you? What prayers, spiritual practices or scripture passages remind you that God is always with you, even in your troubles?

Wednesday 20 January

1 Do you find it intimidating to talk openly about your faith? Does it depend on the situation? Tell about a memorable experience from your life when you shared your faith.

2 Today's writer felt a prompting to start talking about her faith. When have you felt a prompting from God? How did you respond? What was the outcome?

3 Have you ever felt like you needed to have all the answers about your faith? Is it hard for you not to have all the answers? Why or why not?

4 Does following God's guidance get easier over time? How do you make sure you are always listening for God's guidance?

5 How can you share God's love with someone today? What new habits can you begin that will help you share God's love more effectively?

Wednesday 27 January

1 Are you in a place of uncertainty right now or have you been in one in the past? Reflect on those times, and share what you need from God, others and yourself amid uncertain circumstances.

2 How has God shown you that God's love is certain? What does it mean to you that you are guaranteed unfailing love at all times? How does that change the way you respond to life's challenges?

3 When have you experienced God's protection in difficult times? How have you held on to that protection? What spiritual practices help you hold on to God in hard times?

4 Describe a time when you most clearly saw God's provision in your life – physically or spiritually. Describe a time when it felt like God was not providing for you in the ways you would have liked. How did you hold on to and remain close to God each time?

5 Of the three promises today's writer mentions, which one is the most encouraging for you today? What does it look like for you to hold on to that promise from God?

Wednesday 3 February

1 Describe a time when you were on a difficult journey. Did you feel God walking that path with you? How did you experience God's peace and healing during that time?

2 How do you respond when you see others struggling? Does your response change based on how much you are struggling at the time? Is it easier or harder for you to comfort others when you are also in need of comfort?

3 How do you remain aware of opportunities to show God's compassion to others? In what ways can you share the love of Jesus without words today?

4 What scripture passages and prayer practices help you to focus on the needs of those around you? How is God calling you to help those in your community who are hurting?

5 In what ways does your church reach out and show God's compassion to others? Do you participate in those efforts? In what other ways does your church community encourage you to help those around you?

Wednesday 10 February

1 Do you participate in a small group? In what ways have you benefited from the group? What practices might your group implement to help its members avoid distractions?

2 Why do you think Jesus was so good at focusing on others? What can you learn from Jesus' focus? How will you try to follow his example today?

3 List some common distractions that weigh on you before or during a worship service, small-group meeting or devotional time. How can you intentionally avoid those distractions in the coming week?

4 Read your favourite scripture passage containing the phrases 'Jesus saw' or 'Jesus looked'. Why do you like that passage? What does it teach you about yourself, Jesus or others?

5 What helps you to slow down and focus on the present moment? How do you most notice God's love when you slow down in that way? How do you make sure you take time to notice the holiness of those moments?

Wednesday 17 February

1 When have you had to wait for something that, when it came to fruition, was worth the wait? How was that experience similar to what today's writer describes about the broom bush?

2 Today's meditation references the waiting of Abraham, Sarah and David. What other biblical characters had to wait? How do you imagine they felt in that waiting? What can we learn from their situations?

3 Who and what helps you respond to times of waiting with patience and hope? How does your faith affect the way you feel about waiting?

4 When you are experiencing a barren time, is it hard for you to believe that the 'bare, green sticks' of your life will blossom again? What are your prayers like in such times? What scripture verses comfort you when you feel this way?

5 In what ways do you remember the 'blossoms of the past'? What blossoms do you hope people will remember about you, your family, your faith community or your country? Why do you think it is important both to remember what has passed and to anticipate what is to come?

Wednesday 24 February

1 Today's writer initially thought his project wouldn't take long, but he soon realised he was wrong. Has something similar happened to you? Why do you think our first impressions can so often be inaccurate?

2 What areas of your life feel rushed? How might you try to slow down in those areas? What do you think you might notice when you slow down?

3 In what simple ways can you bear someone's burden today? How will you be more aware of the opportunities that God provides to help and lift others up?

4 When you feel like others are too busy to notice your struggles, what helps you find peace and encouragement? What scripture passages do you most relate to in those times? What prayers bring you comfort? What activities help you find relief?

5 Besides bearing one another's burdens, what other actions make it possible to fulfil the law of Christ? How would your life be different if you and everyone around you tried to live in a way that would lift others up, bear one another's burdens and follow the example that Jesus set?

Wednesday 3 March

1 When have you been unhappy about giving up something for Lent? How do you combat those feelings during this season?

2 If you have given up a bad habit for Lent, how was that experience different from giving up something you enjoy? If you have not, how do you think doing so might affect your life?

3 The writer describes a few things we might take up during Lent, rather than giving anything up. In what ways does that idea differ from the ways in which you typically think of Lent? How is it familiar? What could you take up for Lent?

4 How are you looking for new experiences that God might be guiding you to this Lenten season? In what ways do you think you might be better able to experience God's grace and love by trying a new Lenten practice?

5 How does God challenge you? How does scripture or your faith community challenge you? How do you challenge yourself? In what ways do you find growth and blessings in those challenges?

Wednesday 10 March

1 What does 'God's healing touch' mean to you? When have you needed God's healing touch? Where did you find it?

2 Describe a situation where you clearly felt God's love. Why do you think God's love felt so close and powerful in that situation? How were you comforted and encouraged by it?

3 How can you help someone who is hurting? With what loving actions will you remind someone of God's love today?

4 When do you feel surrounded by God's healing love? Who in your life helps you to feel God's presence and love? How do you feel God's love when you are alone?

5 What biblical stories best reflect the power of God's healing love for you? Why? How do those stories encourage you when you are feeling overwhelmed and discouraged?

Wednesday 17 March

1 How does knowing that others can relate to your feelings and experiences encourage you? How do you find community with people who share your feelings and experiences?

2 In what ways are you comforted by knowing that Jesus understands your human experience and needs? How does that knowledge strengthen your faith and your connection with Jesus and God?

3 Which scripture passages best capture Jesus' humanity? Why?

4 Name ways in which you can show compassion and empathy to those around you today. In what ways are you intentional about showing compassion to others every day?

5 Where in your life do you most often struggle to express empathy and compassion? What prayers, scripture verses, spiritual practices or interactions help you in those areas?

Wednesday 24 March

1 What gives you hope when you feel like your situation will never change? Where do you find encouragement?

2 Is it easy for you to pray with full trust in God? How are your prayers different when you are praying with full trust? How does praying this way change your heart?

3 Today's writer was encouraged in her prayer life by her friend. What role have friends played in your faith? How do you encourage your friends in their faith?

4 Who in the Bible trusted like never before? What was the outcome? How does their story inspire you to do the same?

5 Do you believe in God's ability to do miracles? How do you continue to trust in God, even if you don't receive the miracles you hoped for?

Wednesday 31 March

1 When you are in church, do you ever find your mind flooded with worries instead of focused on worship? What helps you to focus on the present moment?

2 Describe a time when someone reached out to you in Christian love before doing anything else. How did that make you feel? What did you learn from that experience?

3 Today's prayer focus is 'Someone I disagree with'. How might praying for someone you disagree with help your situation? What kinds of things might you pray for?

4 What does it mean to you to have a life that looks like the life of Jesus? What do you do each day to try to live like Jesus lived? How does Jesus' example change the way you interact with those around you?

5 When you disagree with other Christians, what do you do to resolve those disagreements? When members of your church family have disagreements, how are those disagreements handled? In what ways does Christian love help in finding a resolution?

Wednesday 7 April

1 In what ways does Jesus' command to love one another and his instruction to make disciples affect your daily life? How do you make an effort to follow Jesus' instructions?

2 How does today's quoted scripture encourage you? When over the past few days have you felt Jesus' presence?

3 Do you find it easy to reach out to others and share your faith with them? How does God help you and give you the strength to do so?

4 Today's writer describes the importance of following Jesus' instructions to love one another and to make disciples. What do you think grows a strong church and a strong faith?

5 In what ways is your church community intentional about meeting new people and forming loving connections with them? In what ways are you intentional about this?

Wednesday 14 April

1 Have you ever used a similar practice of reciting a verse in the morning and a different one in the evening? If so, what was your experience? If not, in what ways might it benefit you?

2 Today's writer finds great comfort in Psalm 4:8 and 118:24. What Bible verses bring you comfort and focus your mind on God's presence? How do you interact with those verses daily?

3 What spiritual practices make your life sweeter? How do you decide what will become a daily practice versus an occasional practice?

4 In what ways is your life enriched when you focus on God's blessings? What differences do you notice in yourself when you are not as mindful of God's love and blessings?

5 How can you encourage those around you to rejoice in the blessings of God's world? Who in your life has shown you a blessing today? What can you do to be a blessing to someone else today?

Wednesday 21 April

1 When you are going through a difficult time, how important is it for you to have someone to lean on? Where do you find comfort and guidance?

2 Today's writer describes her initial prayers as simply kneeling and crying to God. Have you ever prayed to God through your tears? Do you feel the need to speak when you pray, or are you comfortable praying without words?

3 Is it easy for you to trust God in hard times? When has a problem made you trust and rely on God more? Does that bring you closer in your relationship with God?

4 Has there been a time in your life when you didn't want to trust or pray to God? How did you find comfort in that time? How did you come to trust and pray to God again?

5 How important is it to you to use words when speaking to God? When do you feel like it is okay to speak to God through silence? How does it encourage you to know that God will listen to our prayers even when we have no words?

Wednesday 28 April

1. Knowing that your actions reflect back on your faith, how do you try to leave a good impression wherever you go? List some of the intentional choices that you make.

2. Have you ever acted in a way that did not accurately represent your faith? How did you feel about that situation? Were you able to rectify it? What did you learn from that experience?

3. Do you find it easy or difficult to love everyone? How do you remind yourself to love everyone, even when you may be busy or around people you find hard to love? What prayers or spiritual practices encourage you to love everyone?

4. Do you ever feel pressure knowing that you are an ambassador for Christ? Do you enjoy the responsibility? How do you stay mindful of your calling to be an ambassador for Christ?

5. How do you put your best foot forward to represent Christ every day? How do you think your church represents Christ to others? Are there areas you wish that you or your church could improve in representing Christ?

Lent is not about giving up or taking up, but a radical opening up: the opening up of our lives to God's transformative kingdom. That is the challenge Trystan Owain Hughes sets in *Opening Our Lives*, BRF's Lent book for 2021. Through practical daily devotions he calls on us to open our eyes to God's presence, our ears to his call, our hearts to his love, our ways to his will, our actions to his compassion and our pain to his peace.

Opening Our Lives
Devotional readings for Lent
Trystan Owain Hughes
978 0 85746 882 6 £8.99
brfonline.org.uk

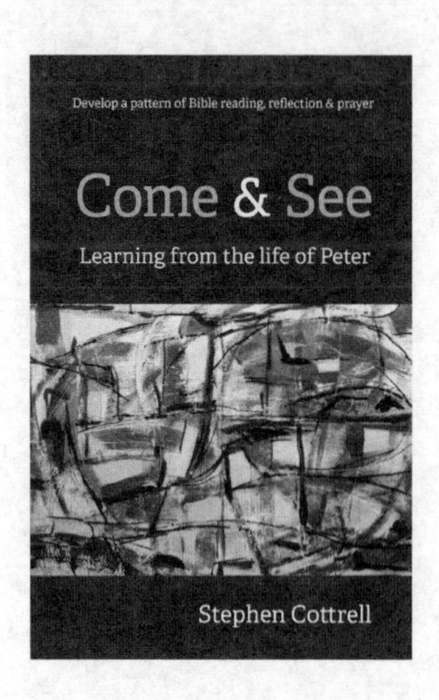

When we look at the life of Peter – fisherman, disciple, leader of the church – we find somebody who responded wholeheartedly to the call to 'come and see'. Come and meet Jesus, come and follow him, come and find your life being transformed. *Come and See* provides a pattern of Bible reading, reflection and prayer based on the story of Peter, plus comment and questions for personal response or group discussion.

Come and See
Learning from the life of Peter
Stephen Cottrell
978 1 80039 019 5 £7.99
brfonline.org.uk

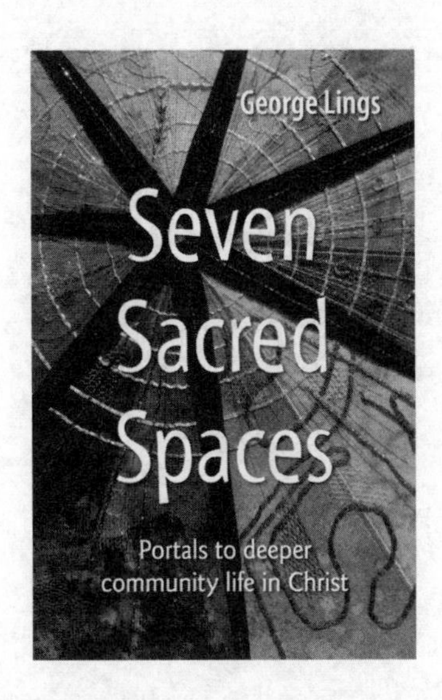

Too often people's understanding of and engagement with 'church' is reduced to corporate worship, when it is so much more. George Lings identifies seven characteristic elements in Christian communities through the ages, which when held in balance enable a richer expression of discipleship, mission and community.

Seven Sacred Spaces
Portals to deeper community life in Christ
George Lings
978 0 85746 934 2 £10.99
brfonline.org.uk

This book is addressed directly to women experiencing domestic abuse, and to those who seek to support them, including pastoral leaders, friends and support organisations. It debunks the myths – perpetuated by some abusers and, unwittingly, by many churches – which prevent women from getting out of harm's way. It helps them realise that the Bible does not belong to their abuser but is a text of liberation. Written with careful attention to pastoral issues, it closely examines and clearly explains the relevant scriptural texts.

The Bible Doesn't Tell Me So
Why you don't have to submit to domestic abuse and coercive control
Helen Paynter
978 0 85746 989 2 £8.99
brfonline.org.uk

Enabling all ages to grow in faith

At BRF, we long for people of all ages to grow in faith and understanding of the Bible. That's what all our work as a charity is about.

- Our **Living Faith** ministry offers resources to help Christians go deeper in their understanding of scripture, in prayer and in their walk with God. Our conferences and events bring people together to share this journey, while our Holy Habits resources help whole congregations grow together as disciples of Jesus, living out and sharing their faith.
- We also want to make it easier for local churches to engage effectively in ministry and mission – by helping them bring new families into a growing relationship with God through **Messy Church** or by supporting churches as they nurture the spiritual life of older people through **Anna Chaplaincy**.
- Our **Parenting for Faith** team coaches parents and others to raise God-connected children and teens, and enables churches to fully support them.

Do you share our vision?

Though a significant proportion of BRF's funding is generated through our charitable activities, we are dependent on the generous support of individuals, churches and charitable trusts.

If you share our vision, would you help us to enable even more people of all ages to grow in faith? Your prayers and financial support are vital for the work that we do. You could:

- Support BRF's ministry with a regular donation;
- Support us with a one-off gift;
- Consider leaving a gift to BRF in your will (see page 152);
- Encourage your church to support BRF as part of your church's giving to home mission – perhaps focusing on a specific ministry or programme;
- Most important of all, support BRF with your prayers.

Donate at **brf.org.uk/donate** or use the form on pages 153–54.

There is a time for everything...

There is a time for everything, and a season for every activity under the heavens: a time to be born and a time to die... a time to kill and a time to heal, a time to tear down and a time to build, a time to weep and a time to laugh...
ECCLESIASTES 3:1–4 (NIV, abridged)

I feel intimidated by the task before me: writing something now, in mid-June, that will still be of substance when you read it early next year. Yet, I have good cause for confidence.

While coronavirus has affected us all, some in ways that will never be forgotten, there is comfort to be found in the words of scripture. Ecclesiastes tells us that there is a time for everything – a season comes, and a season goes. Jesus warns us not to store up treasures for ourselves on earth, but rather to place our hope fully in the heavenly kingdom, where good things do not end and where every tear is wiped away.

These truths do not remove the pain we feel now. They do give hope beyond it.

Our work as a charity is to share timeless truths and an unswerving hope with a constantly changing world – work that requires we adapt to make a difference in every generation.

Much of what we do today – and God willing into the future – is funded by donations and gifts in wills.

I'd like to invite you to prayerfully consider whether you could support this work through a gift in your will. If you would like further information about leaving a gift in your will to BRF, please get in touch with us on **+44 (0)1235 462305**, via **giving@brf.org.uk** or visit **brf.org.uk/lastingdifference.**

Martin Gee
Fundraising manager

PS: Please be assured that whatever decision you reach about your will, you don't need to tell us and we won't ask. May God grant you wisdom as you reflect on these things.

Pray. Give. Get involved.
brf.org.uk

SHARING OUR VISION – MAKING A GIFT

I would like to make a gift to support BRF. Please use my gift for:

☐ BRF charity ☐ Anna Chaplaincy ☐ Living Faith ☐ Messy Church

☐ Parenting for Faith ☐ where it is most needed

Title	First name/initials	Surname

Address	
	Postcode
Email	
Telephone	
Signature	Date

giftaid it You can add an extra 25p to every £1 you give.

Please treat as Gift Aid donations all qualifying gifts of money made

☐ today, ☐ in the past four years, ☐ and in the future.

I am a UK taxpayer and understand that if I pay less Income Tax and/or Capital Gains Tax in the current tax year than the amount of Gift Aid claimed on all my donations, it is my responsibility to pay any difference.

☐ My donation does not qualify for Gift Aid.

Please notify BRF if you want to cancel this Gift Aid declaration, change your name or home address, or no longer pay sufficient tax on your income and/or capital gains.

Please complete other side of form ➡

Please return this form to:

BRF, 15 The Chambers, Vineyard, Abingdon OX14 3FE

The Bible Reading Fellowship is a Registered Charity (233280)

SHARING OUR VISION – MAKING A GIFT

Regular giving

By Direct Debit: You can set up a Direct Debit quickly and easily at **brf.org.uk/donate**

By Standing Order: Please contact our Fundraising Administrator +44 (0)1865 319700 | **giving@brf.org.uk**

One-off donation

Please accept my gift of:

☐ £10 ☐ £50 ☐ £100 Other £ ☐

by (*delete as appropriate*):

☐ Cheque/Charity Voucher payable to 'BRF'

☐ MasterCard/Visa/Debit card/Charity card

Name on card

Card no. ☐☐☐☐ ☐☐☐☐ ☐☐☐☐ ☐☐☐☐

Expires end M M Y Y Security code* ☐☐☐

*Last 3 digits on the reverse of the card
ESSENTIAL IN ORDER TO PROCESS YOUR PAYMENT

Signature | Date

☐ I would like to leave a gift in my will to BRF.

For more information, visit **brf.org.uk/lastingdifference**

For help or advice regarding making a gift, please contact our Fundraising Administrator +44 (0)1865 319700

Registered with FUNDRAISING REGULATOR

Please complete other side of form

Please return this form to:
BRF, 15 The Chambers, Vineyard, Abingdon OX14 3FE

BRF

The Bible Reading Fellowship is a Registered Charity (233280)

How to encourage Bible reading in your church

BRF has been helping individuals connect with the Bible for over 90 years. We want to support churches as they seek to encourage church members into regular Bible reading.

Order a Bible reading resources pack
This pack is designed to give your church the tools to publicise our Bible reading notes. It includes:

- Sample Bible reading notes for your congregation to try.
- Publicity resources, including a poster.
- A church magazine feature about Bible reading notes.

If you require a pack to be sent outside the UK or require a specific number of sample Bible reading notes, please contact us for postage costs. More information about what the current pack contains is available on our website.

How to order and find out more
- Visit **brfonline.org.uk/resourcespack**.
- Telephone BRF on +44 (0)1865 319700 Mon–Fri 9.30–17.00.
- Write to us at BRF, 15 The Chambers, Vineyard, Abingdon OX14 3FE.

Keep informed about our latest initiatives
We are continuing to develop resources to help churches encourage people into regular Bible reading, wherever they are on their journey. Join our email list at **brfonline.org.uk/signup** to stay informed about the latest initiatives that your church could benefit from.

Subscriptions

The Upper Room is published in January, May and September.

Individual subscriptions

The subscription rate for orders for 4 or fewer copies includes postage and packing:

The Upper Room annual individual subscription £18.00

Group subscriptions

Orders for 5 copies or more, sent to ONE address, are post free:
The Upper Room annual group subscription £14.25

Please do not send payment with order for a group subscription. We will send an invoice with your first order.

Please note that the annual billing period for group subscriptions runs from 1 May to 30 April.

Copies of the notes may also be obtained from Christian bookshops.

Single copies of *The Upper Room* cost £4.75.

Prices valid until 30 April 2022.

Giant print version

The Upper Room is available in giant print for the visually impaired, from:

Torch Trust for the Blind
Torch House
Torch Way
Northampton Road
Market Harborough
LE16 9HL

Tel: +44 (0)1858 438260
torchtrust.org

THE UPPER ROOM: INDIVIDUAL/GIFT SUBSCRIPTION FORM

All our Bible reading notes can be ordered online by visiting brfonline.org.uk/collections/subscriptions

❑ I would like to take out a subscription myself (complete your name and address details once)

❑ I would like to give a gift subscription (please provide both names and addresses)

Title .... First name/initials .... Surname ....

Address ....

.... Postcode ....

Telephone .... Email ....

Gift subscription name ....

Gift subscription address ....

.... Postcode ....

Gift message (20 words max. or include your own gift card):

....

....

Please send *The Upper Room* beginning with the May 2021 / September 2021 / January 2022 issue (*delete as appropriate*):

Annual individual subscription ❑ £18.00 Total enclosed £ ....

Method of payment

❑ Cheque (made payable to BRF) ❑ MasterCard / Visa

Card no. [ ][ ][ ][ ] [ ][ ][ ][ ] [ ][ ][ ][ ] [ ][ ][ ][ ]

Expires end [M][M] [Y][Y] Security code* [ ][ ][ ] Last 3 digits on the reverse of the card

*ESSENTIAL IN ORDER TO PROCESS THE PAYMENT

THE UPPER ROOM: GROUP SUBSCRIPTION FORM

All our Bible reading notes can be ordered online by visiting brfonline.org.uk/collections/subscriptions

❑ Please send me .... copies of *The Upper Room* May 2021 / September 2021 / January 2022 issue (*delete as appropriate*)

Title .... First name/initials .... Surname ....

Address ....

.... Postcode ....

Telephone .... Email ....

Please do not send payment with this order. We will send an invoice with your first order.

Christian bookshops: All good Christian bookshops stock BRF publications. For your nearest stockist, please contact BRF.

Telephone: The BRF office is open Mon–Fri 9.30–17.00. To place your order, telephone +44 (0)1865 319700.

Online: brfonline.org.uk/pages/group-subscriptions

❑ Please send me a Bible reading resources pack to encourage Bible reading in my church

Please return this form with the appropriate payment to:
BRF, 15 The Chambers, Vineyard, Abingdon OX14 3FE

BRF

To read our terms and find out about cancelling your order, please visit **brfonline.org.uk/terms**.